# GIVING HOPE

## How You Can Restore the American Dream

## Ira Silver

*To Nancy, Arielle, and Benjamin*

*With love always*

# Contents

# PART I

# Sweet Charity

# Second Chances

We hear a lot these days about the growing rich-poor gap and how it is undermining the American dream. A telling indicator is that hard work is no longer the sure-bet ticket to getting ahead it once was. Millions who struggle to make ends meet have little realistic chance of achieving a better life. And for the rest of us, it's all too easy to believe there's little we can do to mitigate this hardship. We often sigh at the magnitude of inequality, seeing personal stories of misfortune as tiny drops within a huge ocean of need.

*Giving Hope* is an antidote to this pessimism. It outlines ways your giving can offer second chances to Americans who have dim prospects for moving their lives forward without outside help. Even small donations of time or money can significantly improve the lives of those experiencing hard times, enabling them to embark on a path toward success.

Of the more than $300 billion annually given to charity in the United States, 81 percent comes from individuals. And most of this money is donated not by the celebrity philanthropists we often hear about but by people *like you*. About 80 percent of individual giving is by those with annual incomes under $1 million and over a third by individuals who earn less than $100,000. These are indicators that your generosity can provide a critical source of help. [1]

Well over 2000 years ago, Aristotle astutely commented: "To give away money is an easy matter and in any man's power.  But to decide to whom to give it and how much and when, and for what purpose and how, is neither in every man's power nor an easy matter." This book provides tips about where to contribute so that you can give gifts that keep on giving. It identifies 75 nonprofits from coast to coast that efficiently use their donations and have track records of creating access to housing, employment, and educational opportunities.

These charities rarely get the exposure they deserve. Although they do vital work to help needy people turn their lives around, they're small and lack the resources to do the sort of publicity that would enable you to know about them already.

Giving to those who have less has deep roots. The Bible contains over 3000 references to helping the poor. From the Old Testament: "Thou shalt surely open thy hand unto thy brother, to thy needy, and to thy poor, in thy land" (Deuteronomy 15:11). From the New Testament: "And though I bestow all my goods to feed the poor, and though I give my body to be burned, and have not charity, it profiteth me nothing (Corinthians 13: 1-13). Bestowing love and spiritual uplift upon the poor is a requirement for attaining salvation. In Matthew 19:21, Jesus told the rich man, "If you want to be perfect, go, sell your possessions and give to the poor, and you will have treasure in heaven." The Koran frequently mentions the importance of giving to the poor; indeed *Zakat* is one of the five pillars of Islam. [2]

Beyond religious obligation and ethical concern, we also give to gain tax advantages or relieve guilt. Most of us support causes that personally affect our lives, and we often have as much to gain as do the recipients of our generosity. As Booker T. Washington put it well over a century ago, "If you want to lift yourself up, lift up someone else." [3]

A classic study of people who saw a film about Mother Teresa's volunteer work in India found that they subsequently had elevated immune systems. The mere thought of donating to charity activates the same part of the brain stimulated during eating and sex. Giving, plain and simple, is an elixir. [4]

For the past couple of years, I have taught a philanthropy course where I've seen firsthand the powerful effects charity can have on donors. Students read the book in front of you, visit several of the nonprofits described, and decide which ones to support with money they've raised. Because students actively participate in funding change, many leave the course inspired to pursue careers in the nonprofit sector after they graduate.

MY INTEREST IN writing *Giving Hope* emerged several years ago in the wake of Hurricane Katrina. Like millions of other Americans and people around the world, I became mesmerized by footage of the massive destruction. The 2005 storm left 1800 people dead and caused billions of dollars in property damage across Louisiana, Mississippi, Alabama, and Texas. Eighty percent of New Orleans flooded after major levees broke. Approximately 95,000 of the city's estimated 143,000 single-family homes were in need of repair. The government's poor planning for a storm of this magnitude was plainly obvious for all to see. [5]

One aspect of this disaster that particularly caught my eye was how people came out of the woodwork to support the relief effort. An astounding 63 percent of U.S. households donated to hurricane relief the year Katrina devastated the Gulf Coast. The $6.5 billion given by Americans set a record. Habitat for Humanity International alone received $95 million. This enabled its local affiliate in New Orleans to become a leader in the city's revitalization, rebuilding 276 storm-damaged houses in the four years after Katrina.

A hallmark of its work was Musicians' Village. Conceived by renowned recording artists Harry Connick, Jr. and Branford Marsalis, this development of 72 single-family homes provides affordable housing to musicians displaced by the storm. Even though there was significant residential blight in New Orleans before Katrina, in the 22 previous years the local affiliate had only raised enough money to build 101 houses. Its development director told me when I interviewed her almost five years after Katrina that the organization had recently been able to tap a large group of donors who hadn't had much interest in New Orleans housing until the storm propelled the city's inequalities into the national spotlight. [6]

The fact that Katrina had exposed these inequalities is the very reason I visited New Orleans. I went with a curiosity about why greater generosity hadn't been shown toward people experiencing hardship there – and across the U.S. – <u>before</u> the storm. After that trip I became interested in how I might inspire others to help people desperately in need who are not seen suffering on TV or on the internet. This book, consequently, highlights ways we as private individuals can give to mitigate the everyday hardships experienced by so many of our fellow Americans.

My interest in this topic has deep roots. *Tikkun Olam* – "repairing the world" – lies at the core of my Jewish identity. One way Jews mend social injustice is by giving *Tzedakah*. The great medieval scholar Maimonides wrote in the Mishnah Torah – his 14-volume codification of Jewish law – that the highest form of Tzedakah is enabling others to attain skills so that they can provide for themselves; to teach people how to fish rather than giving them fish. This is akin to what C.S. Lewis wrote in *The Four Loves*: "The proper aim of giving is to put the recipients in a state where they no longer need our gifts." This book shows how you can do just that. [7]

Perhaps you contributed to the relief effort after Hurricane Katrina or, more recently, after Superstorm

Sandy. If so, then you know how good it feels to assist people who are both struggling and worthy of help. It is particularly gratifying to aid disaster victims since it's easy to empathize with them. You can likewise experience this same feeling through giving that enhances the quality of life for millions of Americans who, despite their best efforts, have few prospects for moving their lives forward without outside help.

WHEN I WAS growing up, during school vacations I occasionally accompanied my parents during the 20-minute drive to their law office located a block from Yankee Stadium in one of the poorest sections of New York City. While en route, I became fascinated by stark differences between the bucolic neighborhood where we lived and bleak indicators that we were approaching our destination. Many buildings were boarded up and panhandlers were frequently standing on street corners. I was just a kid and had no idea why my eyes focused on these captivating details.

It wasn't until I was a sophomore in college and took my first sociology course that I began to connect the dots. I started to see that those scenes of neighborhood disparity I had taken notice of years earlier were a telling indicator of broader inequalities in American society. Around the same time that I was gaining this insight, I was also beginning to uncover a different kind of epiphany: that ironically I recognize social inequalities in part because I have been visually impaired since birth. Due to my severe nearsightedness, contrasts are particularly striking to me. Just as I fixate on dark branches whistling against the bright blue sky, the existence of poverty in close proximity to opulence catches my eye.

As I write these words, I am struck by the fact that now more than at any other time in my life there are millions of Americans struggling to make ends meet who have few realistic chances of getting ahead without outside help. This is so grossly at odds with cherished ideals we hold about ours being a land of opportunity.

It is no wonder, then, that among the jarring stories which surfaced in the days following Hurricane Katrina, the plight of Tracy Jackson, Jerel Brown, and their four children ages 1, 3, 5, and 7 particularly caught my eye. This family had found shelter during the previous week in the squalid conditions at the Louisiana Superdome and New Orleans Convention Center. Before the storm they had lived in a crowded two-bedroom apartment located in a low-income neighborhood across the street from a housing project. They fled the apartment amidst a fire caused by the rising floodwaters. With their $2,000 in life savings now up in smoke, they literally had no more money.

When *New York Times* reporter Jodi Wilgoren interviewed them at Louis Armstrong International Airport as they awaited a flight to a purportedly better place, they still had on the clothes they were wearing when they had abandoned their blazing apartment several days earlier. They had no idea where they were being evacuated. [8]

*At the airport with all their remaining possessions*

The massive charitable response to Katrina enabled the Jackson-Browns and countless other storm victims to receive temporary shelter, fresh clothing, hot meals, and emergency medical care. Those who donated to the relief effort had every reason to see these people as deserving of aid. They were, after all, like so many others who have been the unfortunate victims of natural disasters – people who, through no fault of their own, suddenly find themselves desperately in need of help. After Katrina, there were pieces of Tracy Jackson, Jerel Brown, and their four children in all of us. A comment posted on katrinahelp.com succinctly captured this sentiment: "I've been to New Orleans, I know people who are living there – it seems more personal. It's Americans. It's me." 9

At the same time, this family's story was unique. Because they had nowhere else to go, they and so many other New Orleans residents stayed in their homes or bunkered in city shelters as Katrina's drenching rains and vicious gusts wreaked havoc. Media coverage of the storm depicted those whom the storm left behind as particularly deserving of compassion since they had lived on the margins of society long before the floodwaters took what little they had. But prior to the hurricane – and again soon afterwards – most onlookers were apt to view such people unsympathetically. When there is media coverage of the poor, it tends to depict them as personally responsible for their own hardships and thus unworthy of others' generosity. The immediate aftermath of Katrina was a rare exception to the norm wherein reporting seldom chronicles the daily hardships experienced by millions of low-income Americans. [10]

In the course of my research for this book, I came to see just how extensively the media shape public compassion toward the needy. Disaster victims and low-income people are similar in that they both suffer from extraordinary deprivation. Yet, journalists typically portray them as night and day. Donors consequently feel inspired to relieve highly publicized emergencies yet are often indifferent, and sometimes even antagonistic, about supporting antipoverty programs. Comparing Americans' charitable response to Hurricane Katrina with everyday giving highlights the disparity between our enthusiasm for mitigating emergency suffering and our reluctance to address the inequalities that lie at the root of this suffering.

I HAD BEEN curious about this disparity for quite some time before Katrina. My first book *Unequal Partnerships* investigated an initiative undertaken by foundations, corporations, government agencies, and community organizations in Chicago to prevent local violence following the 1992 LA Riots. Whereas this initiative significantly expanded summer programs for poor youth, it failed to achieve its stated goal to implement long-term strategies for addressing root causes of violence in low-income neighborhoods.

Soon after completing that book, a New Yorker essay by Hendrik Hertzberg about the 2004 Indian Ocean tsunami caught my eye. He argued that the outpouring of aid did not merely signify a massive worldwide response to a humanitarian crisis. This tremendous compassion – Americans contributed $1.9 billion to the relief effort – also brought into sharp focus how little charity targets other social problems that afflict the same people whose lives the tsunami shattered. As aid poured in, UN humanitarian chief Jan Egeland pointed out that more than 30,000 people die every day from starvation and disease in the very places the tsunami devastated. This means that over any given nine-day period more people in these places die of preventable causes than perished in the tsunami. Yet, starvation and disease do not receive nearly the charitable response that the tsunami got. [11]

Other writers have passionately argued that citizens of affluent nations should give to redress these global inequalities. In the wake of Hurricane Katrina, I started looking at domestic giving through this same lens these writers have used in their call for a greater charitable response to the suffering afflicting the roughly one billion people who live on the equivalent of $1.25 a day. I became curious about the gulf between our incredible altruism following Katrina and our comparatively muted concern about addressing inequalities that lie at the root of what was not just a natural disaster but a tragedy with longstanding sociological roots.

This curiosity led me to New Orleans and Washington, D.C., where I interviewed people on the frontlines of the relief effort. I investigated the charitable response to Katrina in the way social scientists have traditionally studied disasters – by highlighting how they expose key aspects of our social world that are typically hidden from view. I subsequently collected data about Boston nonprofits that are making a significant impact in providing access to housing, employment, and educational opportunity. I interviewed staff at these organizations as well as individuals who have benefitted from their programs. These interviews inform the central message in this book: your giving can make a dramatic difference in restoring the American dream. You can significantly help people who live in conditions resembling those the Jackson-Brown family in New Orleans experienced on the eve of Katrina. [12]

JOHN EDWARDS' BID for the 2008 Democratic presidential ticket was doomed long before he admitted to having an affair with his campaign videographer and to fathering her child, both of which occurred as his wife Elizabeth was dying of cancer. Before these sordid details went public, Edwards had held his own quite well for several months against party rivals, Barack Obama and Hillary Clinton. He built his candidacy on the theme of "Two Americas," highlighting how unjust it was that the incomes of most people had stagnated or declined in recent years while the wealthy were amassing a growing slice of the pie. Edwards spoke passionately about how, if elected, he would make attacking the rich-poor gap a centerpiece of his administration.

There was a lot of substance behind his rhetoric. Whereas after-tax, inflation-adjusted earnings of the "one percent" rose 275-fold from 1979-2007, incomes rose just 18 percent for the bottom fifth of the population. Some corporate executives now make in a single day what it takes the majority of workers all year to earn. Roughly 50 million people, about 16 percent of Americans, are officially poor. This is the highest poverty rate since *before* the war on poverty during the 1960s. In many cities – including Miami, Buffalo, Cleveland, Detroit, St. Louis, Philadelphia, Cincinnati, and Milwaukee – more than a quarter of residents are poor. And millions more who do not live in poverty still struggle daily to make ends meet. Nearly 1 in 2 people live in families with annual incomes less than twice the poverty line. [13]

Even had Edwards not become embroiled in scandal, it's hard to imagine he would ever have been elected president. It was one thing for the Occupy movement, comprised mostly of young radicals, to bring attention to inequality and wealth redistribution a few years after Edwards' campaign. It was quite another matter for a mainstream politician to do so. Over recent decades several federal policies – including privatization of government services, industrial deregulation, cuts in safety net spending, and failure to raise the minimum wage to adjust for inflation – have actually played a key role in contributing to rising economic inequality. [14]

The current political climate is unreceptive to reversing these trends. Record deficits have spurred strong support for curtailing social spending. Fiscal constraints are unlikely to abate any time soon, given the mass retirement of Baby Boomers that looms on the horizon. The federal government will be paying out ballooning amounts in entitlements at a time when the retiree population will be growing faster than the tax base, crippling the government's capacity to undertake major initiatives to redress inequality. [15]

Yet, public opinion is in step with growing media coverage of how our society is not living up to its promise as the "land of opportunity." More than 90 percent of respondents to a 2010 survey indicated they believe the distribution of wealth in the U.S. is grossly unjust. Regardless of how much they earn or their politics, people agree that such a disproportionately large share of resources concentrated among so few goes against the strong cultural value we place on equity and fairness.

Likewise, 70 percent of respondents to a 2011 Gallup poll indicated it was "very" or "extremely" important to increase equality of opportunity so that those who want to get ahead can. This sentiment reflects the alarming reality that for many, the American dream was becoming unattainable. The Pew Charitable Trust compared household incomes of youth growing up during the late 1970s and early 1980s with their family incomes as adults 20 years later. Of those born into the poorest fifth of the population, just 7 percent moved to the highest fifth. In contrast, 34 percent did not achieve any mobility whatsoever. Another 27 percent moved up just to the next highest fifth. For those who started in the second lowest fifth, 45 percent either stayed there or actually moved downward. "A consensus view has emerged," wrote the study's author Bhashkar Mazumder, "suggesting that the United States exhibits much less intergenerational economic mobility than previously thought and appears to be less economically mobile than are many other industrialized countries." [16]

That just 46 percent of respondents to the 2011 Gallop poll said it was "very" or "extremely" important for the government to address this issue suggests a preference for the types of charitable remedies this book advocates. A 2012 study by the Indiana University Center on Philanthropy and Bank of America found that whereas 91 percent of people expressed confidence in nonprofits' capacity to solve problems, only 56 percent trusted the government. [17]

THESE FIGURES INDICATE the moment is ripe for *Giving Hope*. Its encouraging message is that each of us has the power to help people in need achieve successes that would be unimaginable were it not for the unsung work of so many nonprofits across the U.S. Although we have divergent political leanings, directing our giving so that hard-working people can achieve the promise of a better life is an idea around which we can agree. We've long seen charity as a way to offer second chances. Now should be no exception.

The following pages highlight just how big an impact your giving can make. Chapter 2 documents stories testifying to Americans' robust spirit of generosity and illustrating the powerful long-term impacts it can have. Chapter 3 chronicles examples of people who give with an eye to how they can spur access to opportunity. Chapters 4-6 highlight specific ways your generosity can restore the American dream, showcasing the work of Boston nonprofits with track records fostering access to housing, jobs, and education. Chapter 7 highlights the tremendous amount we have to gain when we give hope to others. And finally, Chapter 8 lists by geographic region charities from coast to coast you might choose to support that are making a significant difference in enabling people down on their luck to achieve success.

My aim for you in reading this book is to feel the same sense of urgency to take action that so many of us felt after Hurricane Katrina when we saw photos of people on their rooftops desperately waiting in the blazing heat for rescue crews to arrive. Those photos were the canary in the coalmine urging us to view *everyday* financial hardship as a crisis deserving our charitable response.

*Stranded on rooftops awaiting help*

The notion that those who aspire to get ahead yet struggle to do so are deserving of help aligns with the longstanding value we place on equality of opportunity. It isn't right that our society advertises the American dream as available to all yet leaves so many with little hope for a better life. You can change that.

# 2

# Thinking Big

Joel shudders at what might have been if he hadn't gotten that phone call eight years ago. His life likely would have continued to spiral downward. Yet, now at 33 things are going well. His career as a mentor for economically disadvantaged youth who've dropped out of high school is flourishing; he and his wife saved up enough money to purchase a two-family home; and he's back in school part time, continuing the pursuit of his bachelor's degree that he cut short in his mid-20s.

The call was from Mrs. B, a former teacher he'd remained in contact with. "She had somehow found my number and just wanted to check in to see how I was doing because the last time she had spoken to me I didn't seem like I was doing well. I used to confide in her a lot but I had withdrawn and she was concerned because I had stopped going to school."

When they'd last spoken, Joel was a full-time student at the University of Massachusetts-Boston. He did very well his first year, making Dean's List. But during his second year he felt escalating pressure to help his parents, who were in desperate financial need.

For quite some time, they had struggled on just his father's income as a maintenance worker. His mother did not work so that she could care for his sister who had a congenital heart defect. Their situation had recently worsened after they had fallen prey to a predatory lending scam. When they started lapsing on their house payments, Joel substantially increased his hours at work in order to help them out. This left him little time or energy to focus on his studies.

Dropping out of college signified the loss of one of the two positive forces in his life. It was only a matter of time before the other one would disappear too. His relationship with a woman he'd met his first semester was becoming increasingly strained as he became more focused on helping his parents. When he and his girlfriend broke up, he turned to alcohol. He'd been a recreational drinker since his teens but now he started binging. There were nights when he'd pass out, only to wake up in some strange and unfamiliar place. Although Mrs. B was not privy to any of this, she certainly had good reason to be concerned. Joel had stayed in contact with her for several years after they'd met, but the last couple of years – as things in his life took a turn for the worse – he fell off the grid.

It might seem odd that he would have even been interested in staying in contact with a former teacher. He had, after all, dropped out of high school during his junior year. In his mind the decision was a simple one: he lacked the motivation to do well, in large part because the teachers at the Boston public high school he attended seemed not to care about their students. "They would say things like 'it doesn't matter to me because I'm getting paid today.' People ask if it's really true that teachers say such things. Yes it's true. Sometimes, they get frustrated enough that they don't teach. They'll just give people an assignment to keep them busy and that's it – no learning happens."

This was a new school for Joel, his family having moved from Cambridge after getting priced out of the local rental market. He recalled one teacher not even bothering to give him a textbook until he'd been in class for six months. Even before he began attending the school, he had a sour impression of the place. It had received lots of negative press after the city placed it on probation and withdrew its accreditation. And when he stopped by one day to become acquainted with his new surroundings before starting 11th grade, he discovered a scene of pandemonium. A student had just been stabbed on the front steps. There were ambulances and police cars blocking the building and blood was splattered on the pavement.

So it certainly wasn't a *high school* teacher on the other end of the line that day when Joel was 25. Mrs. B was someone he knew from when he participated in YouthBuild, a nonprofit that runs 273 programs nationwide to help kids like Joel. It enables high-school dropouts to earn their GED and gain valuable skills in the construction trades. He had heard about YouthBuild from his brother-in-law. It appealed to him because of its small class sizes and the fact that each week the students alternated between school and work. Joel applied, was accepted, and began the program the fall after he had dropped out of 11th grade.

Mrs. B was a savior from the moment he met her. "She was the first teacher who ever said, 'you know what, you're smart.'" The fact that she and other YouthBuild staff showed a sincere interest in helping Joel to grow personally made a huge impression on him. This support contrasted with a vivid recollection he had from high school. After he had repeatedly been absent, his guidance counselor called his mother and said threatening things like "you realize if he doesn't come to school he is going to fail and not graduate." Yet, the counselor didn't bother to ask why Joel had frequently been absent or to suggest ways the school might help him. These sorts of encouragement are at the forefront of YouthBuild's efforts to help high school dropouts get on track to succeed academically and develop marketable job skills.

In that phone call Mrs. B expressed concern. Joel had stopped coming to YouthBuild events and had become disconnected from people he'd met during his time in the program and in the subsequent year he stayed on as an AmeriCorps peer leader. "Something about talking to her made me feel bad. It made me feel horrible, like at one point I wanted something really positive yet I wasn't really living it." Soon afterwards, she called again to tell him the YouthBuild site where he had earned his GED had a paid staff position available. She thought he'd be a great fit.

Working there full time over the past eight years has given Joel steady and fulfilling employment in a setting where, prior to the downturn his life had taken, people consistently gave him encouragement and support. Being back in this healthy environment has enabled Joel to get his drinking and other drug use under control. "As soon as I had something that I felt was filling my life, I didn't crave them. I didn't want them. I didn't think about them."

And given the rocky path his life had taken during his early 20s, part of Joel's role since returning to YouthBuild has been to ensure that youngsters who complete the program do not become disconnected from the organization. He is keenly aware through first-hand experience that its efforts to foster sustained life changes among low-income youth must be ongoing. Consequently, rigorous follow-up is now done on each graduate. A staff person contacts them once a month for a year after they leave the program and every three months beyond that. "YouthBuild plants the seed and transformation happens," Joel emphasized. "In one year there are only so many things that can happen. After that, something needs to keep that young person going. Otherwise, they can go back to old habits."

A few years ago he organized a panel discussion to highlight this point. Participants included a student just entering the program, one who was about to graduate, someone who had graduated four years earlier, and a graduate from 10 years ago. "It was intense in that you could see where each young person identified moments in their lives where they could have completely gone back to an old lifestyle and the reason they didn't was because that contact with the program was still there."

Joel has stayed in touch with students from

every graduating class since he's been back at YouthBuild. "There are times on the weekend when I go to bed late – I'm on Facebook and a graduate from 4 or 5 years ago sends me a message saying 'Hey Joel, I know we haven't spoken in months but I'm really going through some stuff. Is there any time we can meet for lunch?' And I'm like 'yeah, let's meet for lunch.' I remember how powerful it was because the program provides that support and outreach. But there are some people who just need a person that does more than that outreach, someone who they can call at one in the morning. There are a few individuals from each class, and they don't abuse it. They know to respect it, but they know that I'm a person they can call when they're just down and out and need someone to be on the other line."

Mrs. B showed Joel how to be that kind of person. He became motivated to move his life forward and help others succeed because she saw he had potential and continually reached out to him. We often view people like Joel as having triumphed over adversity solely by their own accord, but that's rarely the case. They need others to overcome obstacles in their lives.

This book is peppered with similar vignettes of personal transformation. These stories are noteworthy given how many youngsters nowadays are in the predicament Joel once faced. In 2012, when the U.S. unemployment rate hovered above eight percent, a Pew Research Center study reported that only 54 percent of people ages 18-24 held jobs – the lowest rate for this group since the government started tracking such data in 1948. The good news is that there are hundreds of nonprofits around the U.S. that work every day to help at-risk youth move their lives forward. These organizations' efforts are testimony to how your giving can fuel long-term life changes for people who have little realistic chance of getting ahead without help. [1]

THE TRIP TO Houston was harrowing for Angela and her eight family members. Not only was the drive from New Orleans long but the road was overcrowded and the humidity sweltering. They were also feeling the emotional trauma of having to leave behind a home that might not be habitable, or even standing, in the wake of Hurricane Katrina.

Once they were beyond the city limits, they stopped at a store to cool off and use the restroom. While waiting for the others, Angela's mother struck up a conversation with a man who asked if they were fleeing the storm. Angela's son nodded. The man then asked the boy if he was hungry. The boy said yes. The man told him to take his mother and go pick out something to eat. A look of disbelief crossed Angela's face. She turned toward the man to express her appreciation and told him she couldn't accept his generous offer. After all, she wasn't traveling with just her son and mother; there were nine of them in all. The man responded: "I don't care how many of y'all it is. Everybody go up there and get something to eat. Come sit down. It's all on me. Get as much as you want. You know, get something to drink. Get something to go."

The family ate, graciously thanked the man, and continued on their way. When they were an hour outside of Houston, they stopped for gas. As they got out of their cars, they saw a couple with two children. They later learned the father was pastor of the local church. He must have sensed this family's ordeal by the expressions on their faces. He approached and told them he would pay for their gas. He also insisted they go into the minimart and pick out whatever drinks or food they wanted. He not only paid for their gas and snacks, but also gave them some cash.

With the help of these two extraordinary people, Angela and her family made it to Houston much more optimistic about the future that lay in store there than they had been 10 hours earlier when they set out on this trip amidst panic and uncertainty. This family was among the estimated one million people who evacuated their homes as Hurricane Katrina approached – one of the largest population displacements in American history. [2]

In the midst of this massive upheaval, many around the U.S. opened their homes to those needing a place to stay after riding out the storm in temporary shelters – people like Jane and Ed Simpson, who live in a four-bedroom house on a quiet cul-de-sac in Framingham, Massachusetts.

They posted on hurricanehousing.org, a site that matched people offering a place to live with those in need of housing. Jane and Ed got a response from a woman named Ajia who had already come to a nearby town in Massachusetts to stay with another family. Originally from Tanzania, Ajia had for some time been living in Seattle. She moved to New Orleans a few weeks before Katrina to begin a job and evacuated during the storm to a shelter in Texas. Since the family she had come to stay with in Massachusetts had kids and the house felt cramped, she searched for another place to live. [3]

Jane spoke to Ajia on the phone and told her she could stay at their house as long as she needed. A few days later, Ajia moved into the fully furnished basement. Jane and Ed stocked the refrigerator and provided her with clothing and other necessities. Since she was given a pickup truck by the other family, they also paid for her gas. After Ajia landed a job in Texas, they bought her a plane ticket and gave her money to cover a week's expenses while she found a place to live.

When she left, they felt good about what they had done for her. "When you have things that other people don't have and if you can make somebody's life better and give back, why not do that," said Jane. "This is somebody who is suffering and has nothing and since we have so much, what does it really cost to let somebody live here? Nothing. I mean it's not like it's a big imposition to just help somebody out." The couple not only felt content that they had enabled Ajia to get back on her feet; they also appreciated that she had been so polite and gracious in accepting their help. [4]

The magnitude of Americans' generosity after disasters lies not only in how much people give but also in who gives and how. The 2004 Indian Ocean tsunami struck a particular emotional chord with surfers. News of big waves usually gets them excited, but not this time. A group of California surfers, jarred by news of the disaster, initiated a charitable campaign to assist devastated villages in Indonesia and Thailand. Organized through SurfAid International, an NGO that relieves human suffering in coastal areas around the world, this campaign raised $500,000. After the September 11th terrorist attacks, some people's generosity literally came straight from the heart. Donating blood was a way those not directly victimized could feel personally invested in helping people who were. At some hospitals the waiting time for giving blood was several hours. An estimated half million individuals donated a total of 125,000 gallons in the weeks following the attacks. [5]

When disaster strikes, even those who have little are inspired to give – people like Maria Pacheco, a 42 year-old unemployed single mother of two living in Chicago. During the three weeks following the 2010 earthquake in Haiti, she and several others from her church collected food and gathered used clothing to send to victims. Despite feeling the pinch of tough economic times, members of the group – which called itself "Poor Helping Poor" – felt inspired to assist those they regarded as much needier than themselves. "We don't have a job, but we have enough to eat and drink and sleep. And they don't. That's what really hurts," said Pacheco. Low-income households actually give the most per capita to charity among all segments of the

U.S. population, contributing 4.5 percent of gross income. The highest-earning families donate about 3 percent and middle-income families 2.5 percent. [6]

There is another group with few resources that also exhibits tremendous generosity after a disaster: children. Though kids don't have large sums to give, their hearts are as big as anyone's. And they can be quite effective at motivating adults to lend their support too. A few days after the September 11th terrorist attacks, my wife and I drove past a group of teenagers running a car wash with all proceeds going to assist victims. We stopped and waited in line for our turn. Watching these dozen or so youngsters working together scrubbing each car with passion and vigor gave us a glimmer of hope at a time when the nation was mired in the darkness of that awful day. Similarly, after the earthquake in Haiti our kids, 7 and 9 at the time, brought home a flyer from school titled "Read for Haiti." It asked parents to pledge support for each minute their child read the following week, with all money raised going to the Red Cross.

THERE IS NO time when Americans' generosity is more vividly on display than after disasters. Four times since the millennium, total domestic contributions to relief campaigns have exceeded $1 billion. Twenty-five percent of U.S. households donated in response to the 2004 Indian Ocean tsunami, 53 percent to help victims of the 2010 earthquake in Haiti, 63 percent to hurricane aid the year Katrina devastated the Gulf Coast, and 66 percent to 9/11 relief. [7]

These figures are a barometer of our everyday generosity. We donate some $300 billion annually to charitable organizations, which amounts to about 2 percent of gross national income. This is more than any other country and roughly double the average across all rich nations. We give 3½ times more per capita than the French, 7 times more than the Germans, and 14 times more than the Italians. [8]

As a nation we take great pride in our generosity. An astounding 89 percent of U.S. households donate on average $1800 a year – an indicator that charity is as American as apple pie, uniting people of varied and diverse backgrounds. This is something Alexis de Tocqueville noted nearly 200 years ago in his then-definitive account of our culture and mores. [9]

Throughout our history we have generally preferred private over government solutions to social problems. Beginning in the early 19th century, people of means supported an array of private institutions including almshouses, workhouses, benevolent societies, charity organization societies, settlement houses, and social welfare agencies. After Andrew Carnegie and Nelson Rockefeller each amassed enormous wealth during the late 19th and early 20th centuries, they created the first foundations. Charity remained a bedrock American tradition even during the heyday of the welfare state in the mid-20th century. And in the current era of small government, giving is perhaps as cherished a value as it ever has been. [10]

Although our charity produces a wealth of

public good, we need to take a hard look at how we give. Doing so can ensure that our generosity has lasting impacts for the neediest Americans. We must recognize, firstly, that our giving provides relatively few benefits to those in greatest need. A 2007 study by the Indiana University Center on Philanthropy, in partnership with Google, found that less than a third of all individual donations help America's poor. In 2010 total charitable giving rose slightly over the prior year yet contributions to nonprofits that target basic needs fell 6.6 percent, despite the fact that the poverty rate was at its highest level in nearly 50 years. [11]

Since U.S. tax law treats all charities the same regardless of the work they do or whom they serve, donors have no particular reason to help the neediest. The largest contributions go to health, education, and religion. Some of this money aids the poor, such as medical research on asthma or universities providing scholarships for low-income students. Yet these are exception, as are instances when religious organizations provide food or shelter. Though this type of charity gets lots of visibility, particularly at Christmastime, the reality is that over 75 percent of church-based giving supports operating costs and salaries. [12]

People with the greatest capacity to give – those earning more than $1 million a year – contribute less than 15 percent of all charity that aids low-income Americans. Giving by the wealthy mostly goes to institutions that benefit the elite: universities, museums, symphonies, and theaters. Of the top eleven gifts made by living donors in 2005, nine went to universities – the largest being the $206 million George Soros gave to Central European University in Budapest. David Rockefeller donated $100 million to the Museum of Modern Art in New York. Bill Gates made the largest donation – $320 million – to the foundation he runs with his wife, Melinda. [13]

Big donors seldom have personal ties to organizations that assist low-income people, as they often do when their giving helps people more like themselves. "So they give to their college or university, or maybe someone close to them died of a particular disease so they make a big gift to medical research aimed at that disease," commented H. Art Taylor, president and chief executive of the BBB Wise Giving Alliance, which promotes prudent donations and high standards among grant-recipient organizations. "How many of the superrich have that kind of a relationship with a soup kitchen? Or a homeless shelter?" [14]

Something else we need to bear in mind is that our giving to those experiencing economic hardship often exhibits tunnel vision. The bulk of it targets basic needs like food insecurity rather than addressing why people experience hunger in the first place. Over the past few decades, millions of donors have helped build an elaborate network of food banks, food pantries, and soup kitchens across the U.S. In addition to contributing money, they organize canned goods drives, sort boxes of food, and serve hot meals. This network of emergency relief organizations serves an indispensable humanitarian function, ensuring that nowhere in the United States resembles places throughout the world where destitute people are seen starving on the street. In 2009, Feeding America – the largest nonprofit within this network – provided 2.5 billion pounds of food to people who were chronically hungry across all 50 states. [15]

And yet, our charity is bittersweet. We're not nearly as inspired to give in ways that enable low-income people to access the sorts of educational, employment, and housing opportunities that could diminish their need for food relief in the first place. These are opportunities like the ones YouthBuild made available to Joel, the man whose story opened this chapter.

Indeed, the 2007 Indiana University Center on Philanthropy/Google study mentioned earlier found that 2 ½ times more giving goes to basic needs than to opportunity creation. Seventy-five percent of the funds raised in response to Hurricane Katrina went to the emergency provision of food, water, clothing, and shelter; and just a quarter supported rebuilding efforts or programs for improving the social conditions that existed before the storm. [16]

A 2009 survey by the Indiana University Center on Philanthropy asked 10,000 randomly selected adults to choose three statements that best characterized their motives for donating to help low-income recipients. The most common reason, identified by 43 percent of respondents, was to provide for basic needs. Just 16 percent indicated enabling the poor to gain greater access to opportunity as one of their top motives. People are more inspired to give fish than to teach people how to fish. Our generosity typically quick-fixes problems by managing the harm while sidestepping root causes. [17]


I RECENTLY RECEIVED a letter from Feeding America which began: "Hunger anywhere in the world is a shame. But in America, it's a crime. This is the greatest food-producing nation on earth. Yet in spite of our abundance, we still have more than 17 million children who are at risk of hunger." In order for this organization to raise large sums of money, it must convey that hunger impacts us all. And since everybody at some point has experienced the feeling of not having eaten for several hours at a time, we can imagine what it must be like to be chronically hungry.

Propagating graphic images of hunger is an even more powerful fundraising tool. And when photos depict starvation in the developing world, the issue ironically hits even closer to home. Consider how often you've seen a photo like Figure 1, which I received in a mass mailing. Although this child lives far, far away, the widespread publicity of his suffering makes it intimately familiar to us. The close-up photo elicits sympathy for the misery so many people around the world experience on a daily basis. This image evokes the feeling that *not* helping to alleviate hunger makes us complicit in it. Geographically distant suffering taps our emotions in ways it never used to because of how rapidly and widely such images can be disseminated. [18]

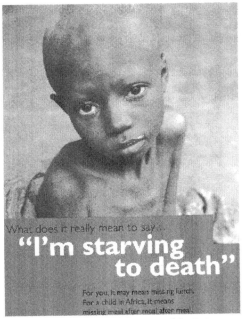

*Fig. 1: Mailing from World Vision*

An experiment done in the early 2000s underscores the point. One group shown a photo of a sick child and told the person's name and age donated over 75 percent more to fund medical treatment for a childhood illness than a second group similarly informed about the child's illness but not shown a photo or given identifying information. Nothing tugs at our hearts quite like stories of adversity we can visualize. We're likelier to help a single, identifiable victim over many faceless people in equal or even greater need. [19]

In May 2010 the co-stars of ABC's *Desperate Housewives* teamed up with ConAgra Foods to organize an online auction with all proceeds going to Feeding America. A couple of months earlier a long list of celebrities including Ben Affleck, Matt Damon, Sheryl Crow, Tyler Perry, and Katie Lee signed a letter from Feeding America urging community leaders and others with influence to get involved in the fight against hunger. [20]

We must recognize how the publicity surrounding hunger defines the moral landscape in which we understand and seek to combat injustice. Indeed, our charitable responses to inequality strongly reflect this publicity. While Feeding America and other hunger-relief organizations do vital humanitarian work, supporting them can preclude us from donating to nonprofits that are tackling the roots of the economic opportunity divide. [21]

Indeed, there is a gulf between the huge amount of giving supporting basic needs like hunger and the tiny amount that expands access to opportunity – a disparity that characterizes what economists Robert H. Frank and Philip J. Cook call the "winner-take-all society." They describe industries like entertainment and sports in which many worthy and talented people compete for a tiny number of lucrative jobs and where those who attain these top positions get the lion's share of the rewards. There are thousands of high-quality college basketball players, yet only a few who will someday get paid millions of dollars to shoot a ball through a hoop.

Feeding America is the Lady Gaga of nonprofits. It's among the relatively few that have the resources to buy address lists and court new donors by mail. These charities can also afford to purchase ad space and hire

PR staff to help get news exposure on *NPR* and in other high-profile media. However, most high-impact nonprofits that are working to restore the American dream lack the resources to widely publicize their good works. They don't have celebrity spokespersons, their work rarely gets media attention, and they have very little capacity to reach vast segments of potential donors through direct mail. These charities that struggle to raise funds to provide housing for the chronically homeless or job training to high school dropouts are like career minor-league baseball players or people who make it to the top 24 but no further on *American Idol.*

Over 85 percent of all giving in the U.S. goes to just one percent of the roughly 1.2 million nonprofits across the country. If you want to think big when you give – if you want your generosity to enable struggling Americans to achieve success – it's crucial that you become more familiar with the other 99 percent. [22]

# 3

# Investing in Opportunity

South Alexander Street is located in a quiet tree-lined section of a mixed-race New Orleans neighborhood that lies perpendicular to where Interstate 10 bisects the city. The houses resemble one another; these "shotgun shacks" were the most popular type of home built in the South after the Civil War.

When Hurricane Katrina made landfall in August 2005, it caused the water level in this neighborhood – called "Mid-City" – to rise over six feet. Most homes flooded; some were beyond repair and eventually razed. Each echoed a unique story of tragedy, loss, and, in many cases, its occupant's quest to return. Dorian, longtime owner of the yellow house at 619 South Alexander, had gotten out of town safely in advance of the storm. She evacuated to Atlanta to stay with relatives, dreaming of someday being able to call her house home again. Yet, like so many of her neighbors she wasn't sure when – or even if – that day would ever come. Her house suffered extensive damage, yet was still standing. Soon after Katrina, an emergency crew removed rotted wood, drywall, and lots of water-soaked personal belongings. The crew also did some patchwork on the roof. But other than that, the house stood idle for nearly five years, exactly as the storm had left it. Mold festered inside.

I visited the home on a sunny afternoon in April 2010. Whereas after Katrina the neighborhood had become a debris-stricken ghost town, many people were now living there again. Yet there was still a long road to full recovery, as half the houses remained unoccupied. The house at 619 South Alexander was just a skeleton of what it had once been. With its interior gutted, it hardly looked like a place someone might call home. At the same time, it was slowly becoming more habitable. Volunteers were inside working, the sound of power tools radiating loudly. A few people were on the porch taking a break from the penetrating heat, which was compounded by the heavy white bodysuits and masks they were wearing. If I hadn't known the purpose of this garb, I might have guessed they were preparing for space travel. The outfits were needed to keep workers safe as they went about the grueling task of removing mold from the house.

Because of their backbreaking labor, 619 South Alexander was finally on the road to recovery. After de-molding, volunteers would put in new siding and windows. Then licensed professionals would install the electrical, plumbing, heating, air conditioning, and ventilation systems. The final stage of repair, again done by volunteers, would be dry-walling, flooring, and painting. Once the house passed inspection, it would be ready for Dorian to return home.

Even though she had waited years for the

reconstruction to begin, Dorian was fortunate to be getting help even this long after the storm. Through word of mouth, she had learned about Hands-on New Orleans, an organization formed in the wake of Katrina that coordinates volunteer projects throughout the city. Much of its work to date had been with groups from around the U.S. coming to the city to repair damaged houses. Many of these groups were comprised of college students experiencing what has become an increasingly popular spring break alternative to beaches, public drunkenness, and wet T-shirt contests. Despite the influx of people wanting to help with Katrina recovery, Hands-on New Orleans had a long waiting list of houses still needing repair. The organization had previously done work in Dorian's neighborhood, which is how she knew to inquire about getting help.

The people working on her house the day I visited were not primarily college students but adults ranging in age from 27 to 52. They were part of a group called Boston Cares, and they reflect the growing appeal in recent years of volunteer vacations. There were simultaneously two other Boston Cares crews working at storm-damaged houses elsewhere in the city. Other volunteers coordinated by Hands-on New Orleans had for a few weeks been working at 619 South Alexander, and a new crew from the HMO Kaiser Permanente was slated to start on the siding and windows after the Boston Cares group left. [1]

I spoke with several of the volunteers at Dorian's house on that hot April afternoon while they took water breaks. Some of these conversations were follow-ups to others we'd had a month or so earlier in Boston, where I learned their reasons for volunteering. In order to make this trip happen, each of them had taken time off from their jobs and had either paid for their own flights or had figured out a way to raise the money.

*Nancy takes a break to speak with me*

Their efforts to contribute to New Orleans' gargantuan task of recovering from Katrina tell a remarkable tale. What stands out is not only that they had traveled from far and wide to fix damaged houses; there were, after all, so many people after the storm who'd come to the aid of their fellow Americans. Rather, what distinguishes those who came in 2010 – as well as the droves of other volunteers who continue to come to storm-ravaged areas of the Gulf Coast – is that they are helping out *several years after* the magnitude of this disaster disappeared from daily news coverage, and hence from the forefront of most people's minds.

These volunteers serve as a model for the rest of us to admire and to emulate. They instruct us that there are problems which compel action regardless of whether the media portray these problems as urgently in need of fixing. The ongoing charitable response to Katrina highlights the opportunity we as private citizens have to take responsibility for investing in solutions to menacing social inequalities that are largely invisible to the public eye. If we can embrace this crucial lesson that restoring the American dream hinges on our making long-term investments, then we will affix a silver lining to the Katrina tragedy.

And we'll also become more personally fulfilled. Kendra, a 2013 Framingham State University graduate who organized a student-run week of service in Louisiana in March 2011 and also led alternative spring break trips to two other locations, commented how working with Habitat for Humanity to build new houses inspired her. "Seeing the devastating impact Hurricane Katrina and poverty were having on people's lives was absolutely moving. Seeing the ruin only gave me the strength and motivation to work on the homes a little harder, longer, and stronger."

Her words underscore that the benefits of contributing to Katrina recovery long after the floodwaters made so many houses uninhabitable go well beyond making others' lives better. Giving to those desperately in need of help greatly enriches volunteers' own lives too. "Participating in service work is not only good for greater society but good for the soul. It allows an individual to feel useful, important and optimistic about the intentions of others.

Volunteering fills me with a sense of duty and accomplishment. Actively participating in a project which improves the well-being of another provides my life with meaning. Every volunteer project I do restores my faith in humanity." [2]

KATHLEEN AND COSMIN'S initial impetus for traveling with Boston Cares to New Orleans in April 2010 was not to fix houses but to attend a friend's wedding. Since they had never been to the city before, the couple wanted to extend their trip beyond the wedding weekend. They could have spent their extra time doing what most visitors do: stroll around the French Quarter, eat scrumptious food, drink hurricanes, and listen to live music. But, Kathleen had other plans. "When I heard about the Boston Cares trip, I felt this was something that was important to do because there is this other side of New Orleans that is still in such rough shape and there are so many people that still need help getting their life back. It did not seem right to visit the one without taking the opportunity to do something for the other." [3]

Just as Kathleen knew that vast sections of New Orleans remained in terrible shape and so many people still needed help getting their lives in order, Nancy similarly felt that too little had been done to revitalize the city. The fifth anniversary of Katrina was just four months away, and yet so many people who wanted to return to their houses still couldn't because repair work had yet to be done. Like Anne, her goal in volunteering was to enable these people to get their lives back to something they could call normal.

Stefanie had previously taken trips to New Orleans to help out, so she knew first-hand that the fabric of certain neighborhoods was still severely torn and that violent crime ran rampant. Courtney, Tracy, and Tim had likewise previously volunteered in areas damaged by Katrina. Tim noted that he had definitely seen improvements from one trip to the next, but he had also noticed how much work still needed to be done. The public perception that New Orleans had been cleaned up and renewed bothered him. He was angered that so many people seemed no longer to be interested in the city's well-being. "I know volunteers who were asked two years ago by surprised friends why they still needed to go back. On previous trips I met many residents who felt that the rest of the world had forgotten about them not long after the news cameras turned elsewhere."

An analysis of coverage in the *New York Times* and *Wall Street Journal* during the 30 days after Hurricane Katrina reveals that reporting about the disaster peaked a week afterwards. By this point, journalists had descended on the scene in droves and were providing stories around the clock. Yet, within a month, the storm's destruction was starting to recede from the public eye, as other events had taken over the headlines. By the time of the Boston Cares trip in April 2010, for several years there had been very little mainstream media coverage of the ongoing crisis in New Orleans, and even less about other storm-ravaged areas of the Gulf Coast. [4]

The city had recently re-entered the national spotlight when the Saints won their first Super Bowl that February. However, the blitz of media coverage mostly echoed the hollow mantra that New Orleans "was back." Now that the Saints finally reigned supreme, the only news stories which seemed to matter were those about how the city had rebounded after years of adversity. Journalists did not seize the chance to present a realistic picture of how the neighborhoods which had been most adversely affected by Katrina were currently faring. Indeed, media coverage after the Saints' victory resembled the local tourism industry's PR during the previous few years. An executive of a sports and entertainment marketing company told *Advertising Age* that "a revitalized French Quarter and the airing of Bourbon Street after the Saints won gave an image into the national conscience that New Orleans is back in a big way. Hopefully it erased some of the lasting images from Katrina for those who have avoided traveling there. New Orleans is a first-rate town for hosting events, and this will only make it better. 5

Given this pervasive image of urban revitalization, the Boston Cares volunteers who took vacation time to repair storm-damaged houses stood out as a unique bunch. Courtney indicated that what inspired her and the others nearly five years after the Katrina tragedy was a concern about "the story beneath the story." She reiterated this phrase several times when we spoke, explaining that the impetus for people to help with hurricane recovery was an awareness of the city's lingering hardships in the years since the storm. She wasn't just referring to the many neighborhoods where houses remained uninhabited; the hidden story behind Katrina was also the stark inequalities that long predated it and which made its effects particularly adverse for low-income people. New Orleans had one of the highest poverty rates in the country at 28 percent. The percentage of poor children was well over twice the national average. [6]

No slick PR could varnish these volunteers' knowledge of such stark inequality. They saw Katrina as a disaster far greater than that ferocious hurricane on August 29, 2005. The storm had uncorked glaring disparities across the city's neighborhoods in terms of people's access to housing, jobs, and education – an indicator that the tragedy had unfolded over many years. This way of seeing Katrina characterizes the broader perspective that there's no such thing as a natural disaster. Hurricanes, earthquakes, tsunamis, and tornadoes disproportionately affect those who already live on the margins of society. [7]

This became obvious in the wake of Katrina. Whereas people who owned cars and could afford to stay in hotels had no trouble evacuating the city, others didn't even have money for a bus ticket – let alone a hotel room – or did not know anyone elsewhere with whom they could stay. Moreover, much of the heaviest destruction occurred in the poorest neighborhoods, yet there was little serious damage to the French Quarter and even less within the affluent Garden District which, unlike most of the city, is above sea level. Although Lakeview, a well-to-do neighborhood built on lower ground, suffered tremendous damage, it has recovered much more quickly than comparably affected lower-income areas.

The day before I visited 619 South Alexander Street in April 2010 my wife, my friend Don, and I drove through Lakeview and then veered southeast through Gentilly and the Lower Ninth Ward. The route was a more-or-less straight line from higher-income to lower-income areas, and it closely correlated with how much recovery had taken place. Some Lakeview houses still showed signs of storm damage, but most had been rebuilt to their former grandeur. Gentilly was more mixed. Like the Mid-City neighborhood where Dorian's home was undergoing repair, some of the houses here had been rebuilt while others still remained severely damaged.

*A rebuilt home in Lakeview*

The Lower Ninth Ward was an entirely different story. People who have repeatedly visited New Orleans since 2005 can testify to how much has changed for the better. For one thing, Brad Pitt's Make It Right Foundation has funded the construction of 76 new homes. But since this was my first post-Katrina trip to the city, I was struck by the overwhelming signs of destruction. Not only were well over half the houses uninhabited, but many appeared as they must have looked immediately after the storm.

A 2012 *New York Times* investigative report revealed how much in the Lower Ninth Ward remained unchanged. Most who evacuated as Katrina approached hadn't returned, and Census data indicated that 75 percent fewer people lived in the neighborhood than in 2000. There were piles of trash everywhere and vegetation grew uncontrollably, in some places over 30 feet above the many houses left in disarray by the storm. [8]

*A ravaged home in the Lower 9th Ward*

During my visit, it didn't take a very discerning eye for me to notice the city's uneven recovery, nor to recognize how it mirrored income disparities across neighborhoods. All it took was seeing this evidence firsthand. Those who have not visited New Orleans since Katrina must rely on journalists and marketers to provide a picture of how the city is faring, both of which have reason to whitewash Katrina's lingering devastation.

The dearth of mainstream coverage about the stalled recovery within low-income neighborhoods reflects the media imperative to report about news that is new and different, which caters to people's short attention spans. Right after Katrina, not only did storm damage fit these criteria, but so did stories of poverty and inequality like the one about the Jackson-Brown family described in Chapter 1. But, with the passage of time these stories were no longer very newsworthy, and certainly not compared to the Saints' first Super Bowl win.

In April 2010, the public reference point for thinking about disaster damage was the earthquakes earlier that year in Haiti and Chile, not a hurricane nearly five years earlier. Given the media's limited coverage of both Katrina recovery and of the economic inequities that magnified this tragedy for the poor much more than for others, it is unsurprising that people who have not seen the lingering damage firsthand would believe New Orleans is back.

DUE TO THE expanding array of 24/7 media outlets, disasters have become big news in recent years. These include cable TV, blogs, text-messaging, Facebook, Twitter, and websites like Disaster News Network and The Disaster Center. Nowadays, it seems reporters move from one disaster to the next. And when there is extensive reporting about a particular disaster, people feel an imperative to help out and aid victims.

A study of nightly network news coverage of the 2004 Indian Ocean tsunami found that for each additional minute of airtime, that day's online giving increased by 16 percent. An additional 700-word story in the New York Times or Wall Street Journal produced an 18 percent rise in daily contributions. "It's out there every day – you can't escape it. It's in your mind and it's in your thoughts. And I think it's because you see and you hear that you just want to help." Carla spoke these words in reference to her recent donation to the International Red Cross during an interview a few weeks after the 2010 earthquake in Haiti. Gwen had given money in response to other disasters, and the constant media coverage of the carnage in Haiti influenced her to support earthquake relief through her church. "When I went on cnn.com and turned on the TV, there was imagery and it was compelling. We are a visual society and I think the actual imagery of people having no home or people crying or whatever the case might be can be very emotional." 9

Major George Hood, the Salvation Army's National Community Relations and Development Secretary, offered these words to CNN's Larry King a few days after Hurricane Katrina. "Right now, we're sustaining life and making sure people are well fed. We're giving them three meals a day; good clean, safe water; and we're housing people – 150,000 people are living in Salvation Army facilities from Texas all the way across to North Carolina right now. And we are feeding 200,000 people on a daily basis." During the segment, viewers saw at the bottom of their screens:

> HOW YOU CAN HELP
> THE SALVATION ARMY
> www.salvationarmyusa.org

In an MSNBC report the next day, Major Dalton Cunningham, the Salvation Army Divisional Commander for Alabama, Louisiana, and Mississippi, soberly stated: "This is one of the most massive disasters I have ever seen in my 32 years of service. It is overwhelming; that's correct. We have 72 mobile feeding kitchens that are stocked and ready and rolling into the areas right now. We have two 54-foot kitchens ready to come in and feed people. They're hungry, they're thirsty, and they need ice."

When the news anchor asked what people at home could do to help, the Major responded: "Well, I would love for you to do two things. One: pray for us and the victims that are suffering so desperately. And if you would like to dial 1(800) SAL-ARMY (the numbers appeared across the screen as he spoke them). You can make a donation over the phone or through our Internet: salvationarmyusa.org." During the interview viewers saw a box at the bottom flashing FEMA IS URGING PEOPLE TO MAKE CASH CONTRIBUTIONS TO ORGANIZATIONS, followed by RELIEF ORGANIZATIONS ASK THAT PEOPLE DO NOT SEND CLOTHING OR FOOD, and finally CASH DONATIONS: SOUTHERN BAPTIST DISASTER RELIEF (800) 462-0657 Ext. 6440. [10]

The Salvation Army, which played a major role in the Katrina relief effort, received $325 million in private funds after the storm, second only to the American Red Cross' $2.1 billion. This is a clear indication that media coverage of relief organizations' progress in responding to the massive humanitarian crisis Katrina produced fed donors' motivations to give. These are the amounts Americans donated during just the first ten days following the four 21st century disasters that received the most coverage: September 11th terrorist attacks – $239 million; Indian Ocean tsunami – $163 million; earthquake in Haiti – $380 million; and Hurricane Katrina – $600 million. [11]

Of the gargantuan amount of total Katrina aid given by Americans – it ranks first among disasters in the amount of private money we collectively gave – 75 percent supported immediate needs via the provision of food, water, clothing, and shelter. There was a similar pattern in volunteers' response. Since so many victims were desperately trying to survive, this humanitarian relief was of course essential.

There's another way to look at this aid. We might focus on the price attached to the fact that news sources play up the urgency of emergency relief after a disaster and seldom give comparable attention to the problems that impede these very same disaster victims' everyday well-being. The media can easily mislead us into believing short-term relief is more important than the recovery work that remains to be done long after the camera crews have left, and more important than mitigating the inequalities contributing to a disaster's uneven devastation. [12]

Some media sources do present a different story than most TV stations and newspapers, and have continued to chronicle the ongoing Katrina crisis. The volunteers I saw working on Dorian's house in April 2010 indicated in prior conversations I'd had with them that they get much of their news from these alternative sources, and that this type of media was pivotal in fueling their desire to help with Katrina recovery. These volunteers actively sought out news about New Orleans from blogs, op-eds, *NPR*, and documentaries. Most had seen Spike Lee's *When the Levee Breaks* and resonated with its harrowing messages. In anticipation of their upcoming trip, they had shared with one another a YouTube clip filmed at the time of the storm's fourth anniversary which depicted how much recovery work still remained to be done. [13]

Following these alternative media gave the volunteers a perspective most news audiences lack. They were able to see why a serious problem needed to be addressed regardless of its lack of media-defined urgency. Feeding hungry disaster victims and enabling them to return to their damaged houses are both vitally important. Yet, mainstream media typically frame the former as more urgently in need of attention and hence more deserving of our giving.

Therefore, in traveling across the country to rebuild houses still in disarray from a storm that had occurred nearly five years earlier these volunteers were voting with their feet. The fact that they were not allowing the power of mainstream media to shape where they put their generosity made them unique. In working to repair damaged houses years after Katrina had receded from the media spotlight, these volunteers highlighted the imperative to address serious social problems regardless of the urgency news reports attach to them. The lesson to take from their generosity is to assume responsibility for doing what we can to mitigate hardships regardless of whether media sources call them to our attention.

IT WAS EARLY evening on a gorgeous day in May. Gazing out the wall of windows from the spacious reception area of the Microsoft New England Research & Development Center, I saw the Charles River glistening in the distance. There was a steady chirm as hundreds of people wearing nametags mingled and exchanged business cards while sipping cocktails and eating passed hors d' oeuvres. For anyone who has attended an after-hours corporate function, this scene appeared familiar; it gave off the impression of being a reception for Microsoft's customers or business partners.

But, looks can deceive. The networking taking place was for a very different purpose than what is typical across Corporate America. People were not here to advance business ideas or their own careers but to promote programs with proven track records of mitigating pressing social problems. Coming from different occupational worlds, the attendees gathered with a common purpose. Some represented nonprofits tackling issues like joblessness, the educational achievement gap, and lack of access to affordable housing. Others had an interest in backing this type of work, and some of them would in time make contributions in the thousands of dollars. These are donors who see their giving as akin to the investments in their portfolios; with the yardstick of growth being tangible evidence of societal benefits.

After people mingled for about an hour, they moved into a large room with screens set up for PowerPoint presentations. Once everyone was seated, the formal program began. Its centerpiece was the accomplishments of a select group of Boston-area nonprofits, most of which worked in some way to mitigate the economic opportunity divide in the United States. One by one, the leaders of these organizations gave crisp three-minute pitches about their work and its impacts. Next, people had the choice to stay and listen to a more detailed presentation or return to the reception area to continue eating, drinking, and schmoozing. As people began leaving around 9 p.m., volunteers at the door asked them to drop their business cards in a box and commit to continuing the conversation with the leaders of these nonprofits in the near future over coffee or a meal.

This annual event – the Social Innovator Showcase – aims to inspire attendees to contribute monetarily or in-kind, or to volunteer their time to support nonprofits that have proven track records of producing significant social impacts. Leaders of the featured organizations do not expect the evening to produce a stack of checks, or even verbal commitments of future support. But, what they can bank on is that the exposure will put them in contact with a new set of prospects and that these relationships can then be developed further.

Each time I have attended the Social Innovator Showcase, I've come away with an unparalleled optimism. The energy and enthusiasm at this event is testimony to how investing in high-impact nonprofits can make tangible and lasting improvements in people's quality of life. Witnessing Boston's social impact market in action for me resembled watching volunteers fixing up Dorian's home at 619 South Alexander Street in New Orleans. Both scenes exemplify small yet significant ways private citizens are assuming responsibility for investing in strategies aimed at fostering greater opportunity for all.

SUSAN MUSINSKY WOULD no doubt be a good matchmaker. She possesses the rare gift of being able to connect people with similar interests so that they can see where their commonalities might take them. Over her career, she has a track record of bringing people together to effect change. As director of Cambridge-based Root Cause's Social Innovation Forum, Susan has been instrumental in forging networks among those interested in being part of the Boston area's social impact market.

The Social Innovation Forum helps local nonprofits with small operating budgets (typically under $2 million a year) to grow so that their work can have a broader reach in tackling underlying causes of complex social problems. Each year it selects a handful of organizations through a competitive process. A team of evaluators cherry-picks them from a field often exceeding 100 applicants. Those chosen as that year's "Social Innovators" are deemed to have the greatest potential for growth in terms of the impacts of their programming and their staff's leadership capacity. Through 2013 there had been a total of 49 innovators dating back to the program's inception in 2003. [14]

Prior to working with the Social Innovation Forum, these organizations have achieved significant social impact yet lack a clear sense of how to communicate the importance and effectiveness of their programs. After being selected, they work diligently over the next several months to improve their messaging. The Social Innovation Forum pairs innovators with executive coaches, consultants, and design professionals that offer input about how to assemble visually sharp PowerPoint presentations. Innovators also get access to a senior-level business executive who offers feedback about the content of these presentations.

By the time of the May showcase, these nonprofits have vastly increased their capacity for growth. Their leaders have refined their ability to pitch the organization's work to different types of audiences in varying degrees of depth. In addition to creating crisp PowerPoints, they have developed a four-page prospectus that concisely spells out for potential donors the organization's problem areas, opportunities for social impact, and how contributions are used. These organizations are now able to convey effectively to any prospective donor why supporting their work is a worthy investment.

"I feel like what it has given us is insight into how our organization is working and the information we need to be more strategic about the work that we do to gain support to develop our program." Toni Elka spoke these words when I interviewed her a week after her nonprofit, Future Chefs, had been among those featured as a social innovator at the 2011 showcase. "They're looking so deeply at our organization that we have to look deep. If you try to do grassroots work, you're engaged in the process and you're putting out flyers or following and running after the work that's happening each day. You don't often get a chance to stop and turn your eye on the real big picture of everything you're doing and what its meaning is." [15]

In strengthening the messaging capacity of local nonprofits, the Social Innovation Forum gives these organizations a stamp of legitimacy in the eyes of prospective donors. People interested in giving can be assured that these charities are not only doing high-impact work, but are also spending their funds wisely. This information is golden given the bitter lesson the nonprofit world has learned in recent years: that a high-profile cause which seems to be doing good work and responsibly using its donations may in fact not be.

In 2011 acclaimed journalist Jon Krakauer published an article and the CBS program *60 Minutes* aired a segment alleging that the Central Asia Institute, the charity founded by Greg Mortenson had committed fraud. Mortenson is author of the international bestseller *Three Cups of Tea*, one of the most uplifting accounts written in recent years about the positive impacts of giving. Or so we thought. For many years the Central Asia Institute had received praise from world leaders who heralded it for building schools in rural areas of Afghanistan where illiteracy runs rampant. But now the organization's Teflon image had lost its varnish. The allegation was that some of the $60 million raised from book proceeds could not be accounted for and that Mortenson had taken credit for creating schools which didn't exist.

Even if these allegations proved to be unfounded, the damage had already been done. They ignited skepticism about the worthiness of giving to charities with humanitarian missions, reinforcing the belief that organizations working for good causes may not be good organizations. These allegations of charitable fraud highlight a concern you may well have about supporting the nonprofits mentioned in this book: whether they are wisely using the contributions they receive. You can rest assured. The Social Innovation Forum vets among nonprofits to identify those that spend money prudently, make a significant social impact, and have a strong capacity for growth. You can be confident that these organizations are good investments.

After being chosen from a rigorous selection process, social innovators work diligently over the course of several months to polish and professionalize their messaging, which makes them even worthier of funders' support. In an annual survey, the Social Innovation Forum has learned that the budgets and staffs of these organizations grow on average 30 percent more during the following year than those comprising the nonprofit sector as a whole.

The experience of More Than Words, a Boston-area bookstore that employs foster-care youth, is typical. When I spoke to its director, Jodi Rosenbaum, two years after the organization had been a social innovator, she pointed to examples of how this experience opened up funding doors. One that immediately came to mind involved "a foundation that we had applied to two or three years in a row and got rejected every single time. Once we were part of the Social Innovation Forum and we applied again, I remember the director coming out and saying that the only reason she was coming to visit with us was because Susan Musinsky had told them to check us out. And once he was here, he got what we were doing and was moved and they've now funded us two years in a row." [16]

There is no mystique about why being a social innovator makes a nonprofit more attractive to funders. "It is all about impact," explained former president of the board of the Anna B. Stearns Foundation, Sylvia Simmons. "We continue to engage in the Social Innovation Forum because we can see the direct results of our support to increase the effectiveness and growth of organizations with missions of importance to us." Jordan Hitch, Managing Director of Bain Capital, concurred that "as an investor who is seeking to make an impact on solving social problems in Greater Boston, I rely on the Social Innovation Forum to identify results-oriented organizations with promise and potential." It is all about the trustworthiness of the investment, according to J. Brian Potts, Vice President of the Fiduciary Trust Company. "The Social Innovation Forum allows us to invest with confidence in dynamic nonprofit organizations that will have a dramatic effect on Boston's future." [17]

With these stamps of approval, you can be assured that the organizations the Social Innovation Forum has vetted are deserving of continued support. And you can be confident that funding these nonprofits will enable them to produce bigger and more significant social impacts. As Susan Musinsky indicated when we spoke, making this type of investment "doesn't mean you can't give to your college or the big art museum, but wouldn't you like to make some investments that might have a chance of kind of getting bigger?"

The take-away here is that we ought to view charity as the gift that keeps on giving. We should expect the money or time we donate will yield measurable returns in the same way that investors set this bar when buying stocks or bonds. From this point of view, for the millions of Americans who are trying to move their lives forward yet aren't getting ahead, it is sensible to create the conditions in which their efforts can pay off – both for them and for society as a whole.

Chapters 4-6 chronicle the work of Boston nonprofits that are investing in housing, employment, and educational opportunity. The Social Innovation Forum has vetted these organizations, so you can trust they use their contributions efficiently to change lives.

These are among the 75 high-impact nonprofits across the U.S. described in Chapter 8. The others listed are also doing work worthy of your support because they have been vetted by donors who fund successful entrepreneurial nonprofits.

THE PEOPLE I saw working tirelessly to de-mold the house at 619 South Alexander Street were glad they'd made the trip to New Orleans, and not primarily because in the evening some went out to eat crawfish and hear live jazz. More importantly, all of them could see their labor was making a difference, enabling Dorian to move a step closer to returning home.

Of course, all it took was a brief glimpse across the street to notice other damaged houses that still sat idle awaiting work crews. Much more rebuilding remained to be done in this one neighborhood alone. Some of those I spoke with intimated they'd be back for another stint of volunteer work. They had become invested in helping out for a reason that went well beyond the fact that the people benefiting from their labor had been victims of a media-spotlighted disaster. These volunteers were motivated by a desire to provide a decent place to live for people like Dorian who had experienced an opportunity divide long before Katrina's floodwaters made their houses uninhabitable.

Several hours after visiting her house in New Orleans, I flew back to Boston. As my flight ascended to 35,000 feet, I reflected upon my time in the Crescent City – what I had experienced and what it meant.

Amidst my pessimism at witnessing stark evidence of the ongoing Katrina crisis was an optimism instilled by these volunteers I had seen hard at work. It occurred to me that their response to this tragedy could be an inspiration for others. Here, after all, were people addressing a serious problem even though mainstream media sources were not publicizing this problem as urgently in need of fixing.

These volunteers' efforts, I thought to myself, could become a model for others to emulate, as well as a declaration that America's economic opportunity divide could be reversed. By following their lead we could embrace the long-term outlook that is so critical for making headway in redressing this problem. We just need to know where to put our resources, which the next three chapters address. With this information in hand, we can help more people gain access to the American dream.

After spending the first hour of the flight jotting down notes about my trip, I put my laptop away and sat back. I started thinking that maybe all the recent hype after the Saints' Super Bowl victory wasn't so far-fetched after all – that despite the evidence I saw of massive rebuilding work yet to be done, New Orleans had rebounded quite a bit from the Katrina disaster and was coming back. With this soothing thought in my mind, I drifted off to sleep.

An hour later I landed and made it home uneventfully. The next morning I heard on the radio that shortly after my flight had departed the previous evening – April 20, 2010 – the Deepwater Horizon oil rig exploded 40 miles off the Louisiana coast. I felt a pit in my stomach at the thought that another disaster was unfolding in the very place I had just been. Amidst my sense of gloom that the region would again be engulfed by tragedy, I felt a dim ray of hope that in time this disaster might also have a silver lining.

# PART II

# Seeds of Change

# 4

# Returning Home

"I used to be a vile and despicable creature," 66 year-old Dane told a packed audience as he recounted the dramatic turns his life had taken. "You couldn't set anything down and turn your head, for it would be gone. I spent most of my life as a taker. Everything was about me; others were just a means to my end. But now if you drop your wallet I'll pick it up, call you, and give it back. And it gives me great joy and pleasure to do so."

Dane didn't have this kind of perspective years ago when he was in his early 30s. He thought he had it all, and in many ways he did. He worked full-time, was married, had two children, and owned a home. But he and his wife fought constantly, to the point where neighbors started calling the police to express concern about the kids' safety. His wife eventually got a court order stipulating that the next time he threatened her he would have to move out. And sure enough, Dane was soon living alone in a Boston apartment he described as "a little square box." He had become estranged from his family and was falling into despair.

He didn't have much in his life besides his job driving a taxi for 12-hour shifts seven days a week. Sometimes, he would hang out with other cabbies playing music, and on occasion they would snort cocaine. The other shoe started to drop when one of them introduced Dane to freebasing. "It was the greatest thing since ice cream. I didn't care about girlfriends, I didn't care about sex. All I cared about was that white rock – that was my God."

Over the next several months his life took a rapid downward turn. Whatever money he earned, he spent on drugs. At the end of his shift, rather than fill the gas tank he would drive back to the garage on fumes. He concocted one lie after another to explain to his boss where the money had gone. Not long after that, the police revoked his driver's license. When he subsequently lost his job, he could no longer afford to pay rent. The man who just a few years earlier had a secure and stable life was now homeless.

He slept anywhere he could – on rooftops, in the entryway of buildings, on park benches, and on the street. His singular mission was to figure out how to get money to buy cocaine. "I became a savage creature; I was breaking and entering every night. The police called me a one-man crime wave."

Dane was no newcomer to theft. As a teenager, he and his friends often stole cars to joyride. He did three short stints in prison before he turned 19, and was later sentenced to six years in a federal penitentiary for driving a stolen vehicle across state lines. Yet now, his indiscretions carried much greater consequences. He was no longer a youngster who broke the law just to have a laugh with his friends. He was nearly middle age, cut off from his family, jobless, and trapped by addiction. His life had hit rock bottom seemingly with nowhere else to go. He remained homeless for the next 24 years, serving several terms in prisons during that period.

While he was sitting on a park bench one day in July 2009, Dane noticed a police officer approaching him on foot. Over the years he had become skilled at trying to evade the cops, but this time he felt no need to retreat since he knew he hadn't done anything wrong. Indeed, the officer wasn't there to arrest Dane but to help him. The man was part of the local police department's homeless outreach division, and told Dane about an organization called HomeStart. Since it was founded in the mid-90s, this Boston nonprofit has enabled nearly 5000 people in situations like Dane's to move into permanent housing.

Because he was both elderly and disabled, within two months Dane got the keys to his own place, a studio apartment in Harvard Square. He vividly remembers the date: September 29, 2009. "I walked in and set down my bedroll and my backpack and I lay down on the floor and used my backpack as a pillow, looking out both huge windows at Harvard University and this gold-domed church. I said to myself 'This is *my home*. This is where *I live*. People around me are paying $2500 a month rent and I'm paying $50 a month for Cambridge housing.'"

HomeStart not only offered Dane a place he

could call his very own; it also helped him get access to other types of assistance. His housing advocate expedited his application for SSI disability benefits, and with that money he was able to buy musical equipment. The advocate arranged for HomeStart to pay the fee to allow him to perform on street corners and in subway stations. He plans to record a CD for sale when people hear him play. Like so many others who have moved from homelessness into permanent housing, getting his own set of keys has been a springboard for making other improvements in his life.

Perhaps the most valuable thing HomeStart gave Dane is a platform for telling his life story. He is part of the Homelessness Speakers' Bureau, which educates people about the myths and realities of homelessness. On many occasions he has mesmerized audiences with his colorful narrative. Speaking publicly not only enables him to earn income; it also contributes to his self-worth. After all, a person must be comfortable with the trajectory his life has taken in order to speak publicly and openly about it. "It's a wonderful feeling to talk about my life. It's a warm blanket that comforts me; I just wrap myself in it."

He much prefers this warmth to the chill that used to run through his veins as he desperately did whatever it took to get his next fix of cocaine. About a year and a half before he moved into his own place, he succeeded in kicking the habit. He was in the hospital after losing his toe because of something stupid he did while high. Being cooped up in bed gave him time to think about this ridiculous injury and to reflect upon a message he had heard repeatedly in substance abuse support group meetings over the years: *first the man takes the drug but then the drug takes the man.* He looked down at his foot and stared at how he had literally given a piece of himself to cocaine. He knew he had to quit or he would just keep giving more. It was a moment of epiphany for him.

Today, Dane is drug-free and living in his own place. He feels whole in a way he never has before. "I used to visit friends and at the end of the month when I had to leave, I would step back on the sidewalk and at that moment it didn't matter which way I turned. But now when I step out on that sidewalk, I know exactly which direction I'm going. And I have the keys in my pocket that represent my musical instruments and other things of value. Before, I used to have to hide my stuff in the bushes. But today I am a whole person." [1]

BETWEEN 2.3 AND 3.5 MILLION Americans experience homelessness at some point during the year, and some 700,000 are homeless on any given day. For most, this is temporary. With little or no help, they're living under a roof again within a couple of days. Yet, about 100,000 individuals are, like Dane once was, chronically homeless. They have either been continuously without a home for at least a year or have experienced four or more episodes of homelessness in the past three years. These people, about 75 percent of whom are men, have fallen on such hard times because of a combination of bad choices and tough circumstances. In addition to being poor, many are also disabled, sick, or mentally ill. Most suffer from a drug or alcohol addiction. Because of these obstacles, the chronically homeless are powerless to change their lives without outside help. [2]

Despite the significant barriers these people face, their lives can be made better. They just need the opportunity to move into a home they can call their very own. Many of the nonprofits across the U.S. addressing chronic homelessness are doing just that. Some embrace a "continuum of care" approach. They work with chronically homeless individuals to overcome obstacles in their lives – for example, by undergoing substance abuse or mental health treatment – so that they're ready for permanent housing. Other nonprofits take a more innovative "housing first" approach, which is based on the notion that having a place of one's own is the key anchor for positive life changes. People are given a permanent place to live without first having to show readiness.

For both approaches, social workers do outreach on the streets and at shelters to seek out candidates for permanent housing. Once the new tenants get their own set of keys, they become responsible for covering a portion of the rent. They pay 30 percent of their income – which often comes from disability benefits and sometimes from employment – while the nonprofit picks up the rest. [3]

Offering a home to people who have spent years living on the streets or in shelters has tremendous psychological payoff. For starters, just having a space to sit and think without others around provides a powerful motivator for a person to want to move their lives forward. Moreover, since these formerly homeless people are now accountable to a landlord, they feel invested in taking care of their homes and empowered to succeed. People get paired with a case worker who makes periodic home visits to help address their individual needs through the provision of social services. These include disability benefits, drug & alcohol counseling, mental health treatment, and Medicaid. [4]

FRANKIE HAS NO memory of 20 years of his life when he was homeless and addicted to drugs. He was often involved in gangs, served several stints in prison, and lost contact with his kids. He also contracted Hepatitis C and developed several other ailments.

*Frankie*

Chronic health problems are the norm for people who are homeless for extended periods of time. In addition to hampering quality of life, these problems also place a significant burden on public resources. The 4800 chronically homeless people who live in Los Angeles, often dubbed America's "homeless capital," incur far greater medical expenses – from emergency rooms visits, psychiatric care, and drug treatment – than do the other 90 percent of the city's homeless population. [5]

In 2006 journalist Malcolm Gladwell wrote an article about a man he called "Million Dollar Murray" who had spent 10 years as an alcoholic on the streets of Reno. In that time, he had racked up higher medical bills than any other person in Nevada! As in LA, even though people like Murray are a small segment of the local homeless population, they are by far the most expensive to support. Due to repeated hospitalizations, doctor's fees, and substance abuse treatment, Murray cost taxpayers over a million dollars. His story cast a dark shadow on the futility of longstanding efforts municipalities had undertaken to manage chronic homelessness through temporary emergency shelter. However, Frankie's transformation shines a bright light on how we can – and why we must – solve this problem, by investing in nonprofits that provide access to permanent housing. [6]

After living on the streets for two decades, Frankie learned about a housing first program for homeless men in Worcester, Mass. sponsored by the Massachusetts Housing & Shelter Alliance. Root Cause recognized this nonprofit in 2010 as a social innovator for the transformative work its *Home & Healthy for Good* initiative was doing to combat chronic homelessness. As of June 2012, it had provided permanent housing and coordinated social services to 582 individuals across the state. Roughly 90 member agencies participate in this initiative, including the one that helped Dane: HomeStart. [7]

Frankie and the other men in the Worcester housing first program each occupied their own room in a three-story building. After moving in, he quickly felt the benefits of having his own space. He began to want to make changes in his life. "It's the most basic idea. It's Maslow's hierarchy of needs," the Massachusetts Housing & Shelter Alliance's Development and Communications Director Erin Donohue told me. She was referring to psychologist Abraham Maslow's theory that people must first have their essential physiological needs met before they can focus on other needs like accomplishing personal goals. "So how do you address your mental health, your physical disabilities, all of these problems if you don't have the same place to lay your head every night? Housing first basically says 'we will give you this unit no strings attached.' And what we find is that when people are given the opportunity for this self-determination, instead of 'you can't drink, you can't do this, you can't do that,' they all of a sudden take ownership and it's empowering." [8]

Frankie earned the respect of his housemates and was given the responsibility of keeping an eye on other residents, reporting any problems to case managers. He also started working toward an addiction counselor education program at a nearby university, and upon graduation passed the test to become a certified alcohol and drug abuse counselor. He now works full-time at a recovery house for Latino men and lives in an apartment with his girlfriend. And the successes of housing first in Worcester go well beyond

Frankie. From 2008-11, the program he participated in secured permanent housing for nearly all of the city's chronically homeless population. 9

"I WAS BROUGHT up in Cambridge, MA by my mother and stepfather, who adopted me when I was in the second grade. From then until I was 13, he sexually and spiritually destroyed me. So I ran away from home. I went to the bus station and got on a bus to New York City with no home, no money, no nothing. I didn't know where I was going to eat, live, or sleep."

People in the packed auditorium sat silently with looks of disbelief as Cheryl recounted how, from a tender age, her life unraveled. Now 63, she was standing in front of a group of strangers shamelessly sharing in vivid detail the tough breaks she had endured over the years. Her courageous presence on that stage as part of the Homelessness Speakers' Bureau was a sign that she must somehow have turned her life around. And she only could have done so by first developing the belief that change was possible, which happened because she got outside help. Cheryl proceeded to describe how getting the opportunity to move into her own home became a springboard for her ongoing recovery from drug & alcohol addiction.

In the several decades before she got that opportunity, her life spiraled downward. "I met a man in Port Authority in New York and he showed me how to get some money. That was through prostitution. So, at 13 that's what I started doing. If I didn't make enough money, I got beat. I've had several broken bones – broken arms, broken legs, you name it. This went on for many, many, many years."

"At 13, I also picked up my first drink and my first drugs. And I started shooting heroin because that's what the man who I chose to be with – that's what he did. And I used to ask him, 'what are those marks on your arms?' He'd say 'well I had a blood test.' And I was very, very naïve. He never allowed me to talk to anybody, have conversations with anybody. As long as it was about the money, that was okay. I shot dope for many, many years in New York. I got addicted to crack, mescaline – I did it all."

Cheryl became a junkie with a habit she could ill-afford. She was also living way beyond her means, eating in fancy restaurants and wearing mink coats. Such luxuries seemed so alluring given the fast cash that came from turning tricks. She had not only become accustomed to this lavish lifestyle but also to sharing it with the man she was involved with, despite the fact that he was abusing her.

After years living this way, Cheryl broke away, returning to Boston nearly penniless. This is all too common for women who flee domestic violence. They often leave in the middle of the night with little but the clothes on their backs. Cheryl couldn't afford to pay rent, so she crashed with people she knew. "But what I would have to pay is my drugs. I had to give them all my drugs and then I could stay, which meant sleeping on the floor or sleeping in a chair."

More often, she slept underneath a bridge beneath the expressway that bisected the city. "In the wintertime, let me tell you – it was cold. It was so cold. I never knew who I was gonna wake up next to or what I had done because I was a different person on the drugs." Cheryl's situation was typical of the roughly 25,000 women in the U.S. who are chronically homeless. A Massachusetts study found that 92 percent have experienced physical and/or sexual abuse at some point in their lives, and that this is a major contributing factor to their being homeless. [10]

She lived on the streets for several years until one day she met a housing advocate from Pine Street Inn, the largest organization serving Boston's homeless. The advocate impressed upon her that her life could become better. "I could get clean clothes. I could sleep in a bed with clean sheets. I could actually have a shower. I hadn't worn clean clothes for months. My pants would stand up in a corner; that's how dirty they were. They gave me clean pajamas, a clean robe, slippers – I mean I thought I was in heaven, especially given where I had come from."

At first, Pine Street Inn offered Cheryl a safe and warm alternative to living on the streets. To secure a bed for the night, she had to put her name into a bucket by 3:30pm. Bed tickets were distributed beginning at 3:45. In time, she learned about a work program in housekeeping at a local hotel that, if she participated regularly, would guarantee her a bed without having to put her name in the bucket.

After working in the program for a year, Cheryl

learned that her housing advocate had submitted her name for eligibility to receive permanent housing. "When I found out that's what my advocate had done and she told me I could move into my own place, let me tell you – people take for granted so much. And when I say that I mean my key is the first thing that opened my door – nobody else's, it was *my* door. I sat on the bed and I felt the furniture – I mean, somebody must have thought I was a loony-toon. I felt the furniture and said, 'This is mine. This is really mine. Thank you, God. Thank you for that advocate.'"

After moving in, Cheryl successfully worked to conquer her drug & alcohol dependency. "I choose to be around sober people today. That's my choice. But believe me – I will help any suffering addict out there." She also proved herself to be such a hard-working and reliable housekeeper that she got promoted to room supervisor – quite a feat for a woman who didn't go to high school and who had experienced long-term abuse.

Her occupational success, like Frankie's, is noteworthy given the hurdles that remain even after chronically homeless people move into their own homes. "Employment is tricky because in reality the majority of folks we're dealing with have been homeless for years and years," said the Massachusetts Housing & Shelter Alliance's Erin Donohue. "So truth be told, in a lot of cases they're not going to be fully employed functioning people. But what they can do is get to a point where maybe they can do some part-time work, or they can do some volunteering. But, for the most part they have so many disabilities that a lot of the work is focused on getting their health back in order really and putting their lives back together after years of being homeless." So although Cheryl and Frankie's employment successes aren't the norm, their stories reveal what is possible when a chronically homeless person moves into permanent housing.

In this regard, it's telling that Pine Street Inn has recently shifted its longstanding response to homelessness. For years after its founding in 1969, the primary aim was to provide temporary shelter; 70 percent of its beds used to be for emergency use and 30 percent for permanent housing. But because housing first has transformed so many lives while also saving money, the proportion has shifted to 50/50 and in the next few years the goal is to move to 30/70. This change reflects the broader policy stance nonprofits and government are taking nowadays toward homelessness: that moving individuals like Cheryl, Frankie, and Dane into their own homes not only fuels positive life changes but also frees up emergency beds for those whose needs are truly temporary. These are people who are homeless due to an immediate housing crisis and are likely, with just a little bit of short-term help, to get back under a roof within a day or two.

Cheryl finished her story by discussing her children. Earlier, she'd indicated giving birth to two kids a year apart when she was in her early 20s. But since life as a junkie made her unfit to parent, she was forced to give them up for adoption. In her early 30s she had another child, but lost contact with him as her life spiraled downwards. Given how riveting this was to hear, Cheryl's final words were a sure sign that she had moved her life forward since getting her own place.

"My three children – all three of them are back in my life. One is 43, the other one is 42, and the other one is 33. They're all in my life today, by the grace of God. So, thank you for letting me share." [11]

PETER LOVES TO paint. He has 3-5 pieces in progress at any given time. At 81 he's going strong and is busily at work during most waking hours. His beautiful creations adorn the walls of his one-bedroom apartment from floor to ceiling.

Peter isn't exactly the sort of person who comes to mind when we think of the chronically homeless. When he was younger, he was a teacher for many years in Springfield, Mass. and in his spare time he painted. A longtime smoker, in 2006 he was diagnosed with lung cancer. The doctor told him it would likely be terminal. While contemplating his next move, Peter heard about a new clinical trial being undertaken at the Dana-Farber Cancer Institute. So, in 2007 he moved to Boston to participate in it.

*Peter*

Believing his days were numbered, Peter made the radical decision to give away all his possessions. "I started with the car – I gave that to a young lady who was 16 years old. I came to Dana-Farber with the clothes on my back and they said to me 'where are you staying tonight?' I looked at them astounded and I said 'I'm staying in your hospital.' And they said 'We don't have a hospital.' So they put me in a cab with some coupons and off I went to Shattuck Shelter – a homeless shelter."

"It was the wintertime. I didn't relish the idea of sleeping on a bench." So this onetime middle-class man who had worked hard for many years was now inhabiting a room with 100 other men and having to shower without privacy. "Living in a shelter, they take away something which is very important. They don't mean to take it away; it just disappears. It's your own worth. People want to be known that they have worth. It's very important – that I am somebody." For Peter, being homeless was not only psychologically difficult but also exacerbated medical complications from daily radiation and being a long-term diabetic.

He stayed at the shelter almost a year while undergoing treatment. Incredibly, his cancer went into full remission. Moreover, a social worker from the nonprofit organization Hearth told him more good news. He had cleared the waiting list and would soon be receiving his own apartment. He was placed in Spencer House, a recently constructed four-story brick building of affordable elder housing in the city's Roxbury neighborhood. Each of the 46 one-bedroom apartments is heated, air-conditioned, and has a kitchen and private bathroom.

Root Cause recognized Hearth as a social innovator in 2009 for its work in providing permanent housing to Boston's elderly homeless population. The organization assists anyone over 50 living on the streets or in shelters. This is approximately 1200 people, a third of Boston's adult homeless. Each week, case workers visit 10 area shelters to forge and build relationships with elderly homeless and provide information about how they can attain a permanent place to live. Case workers assist with the detailed process of applying for subsidized housing, which can take over a year. During this time, they also help the individual get access to necessary services including medical, dental, and mental health care; substance abuse treatment; disability and veterans benefits; legal aid; and financial help.

When housing becomes available, the case manager accompanies the new tenant to the lease signing and assists with moving in, furnishing the apartment, and setting up utilities. The case worker also helps the tenant access public transportation, get acclimated to the neighborhood, and develop a plan for healthy eating. And their relationship doesn't end there. Each tenant and social worker devise a customized case management plan to ensure that the tenant will receive whatever services might be needed in the future.

The people Hearth serves tend to be, in clinical terms, considerably more aged than their years. Housing insecurity exacerbates typical characteristics of growing old (frailty, chronic disease, impaired mental function, and social isolation), accelerating the aging process. Hearth's work is especially vital when we consider that across major metropolitan areas, the elderly homeless population has grown 32 percent since 1990. It's expected to increase a third by 2020 and to double by 2050.

Yet seniors remain an overlooked group. Hearth is the *only* organization in the U.S. with the sole aim to end elder homelessness. And it is producing significant results, having helped approximately 1500 seniors attain permanent housing since its founding in 1991. Over 96 percent of the people it places maintain their housing for at least a year, far surpassing the expected 71 percent retention rate after six months set by the federal government's Department of Housing and Urban Development.

Like Peter, most of Hearth's recipients move into city-operated buildings. The organization also manages 196 units at eight of its own properties. When I visited the site in Boston's South End, my jaw dropped. The building was brightly lit and clean. The dining room and community rooms were tastefully furnished and decorated. There were potted plants scattered about and a rooftop garden where, with help from volunteers, residents can grow flowers or vegetables. Even more impressive are the services offered. At this site, as well as at each of the seven others, a staff of nurses, social workers, activity directors, resident coordinators, and personal care homemakers is available 24 hours a day. Their aim is to foster residents' self-sufficiency and independence while providing whatever services individuals may require.

What struck me the most during my visit was the realization that residing here offers the opportunity to be part of a community and live a full, active, and fulfilling life. It is a place where a person can regain a sense of self-worth after having been physically and psychologically bruised by spending significant time on the streets or at shelters.

Having his own place gave Peter a new lease on life, offering him solitude and the chance to return to what he loved to do. It was only a matter of time before his artwork captured the interest of other residents. "I did the first batch of paintings – 40 of them – and then I said to the other people 'do you want a painting? It's free. You come into the apartment and pick out something.' And that's exactly what they did. Everybody wanted flowers. My God, I never painted so many flowers in my life." He prefers to paint abstracts.

Peter not only gave away artwork to his neighbors but also started offering them painting and jewelry-making classes. He was keenly aware from firsthand experience how easily homelessness strips people of their dignity, and recognized that he had something to offer to help others feel important again. "They look at the mirror and say 'Jesus, who am I?' They lose their identity. This (teaching them a skill) gives them an avenue for worth."

The buzz around Peter's artwork kept growing. In addition to offering free paintings to his neighbors, he also began giving them to Hearth to display and auction. With the organization's help and publicity, he held several art shows in and around Boston in 2008 and 2009. In total, he donated 120 paintings, raising about $10,000 for the organization. [12]

IT SIMPLY ISN'T right that some people lack a key building block for a decent life: a place of their own. Housing should be regarded as a basic human right. In 2010, the federal government embraced this principle when it released a plan calling for an end to chronic homelessness. The plan was based on clear evidence that this problem is solvable. Nationwide, chronic homelessness fell 30 percent from 2005-09 and another 11 percent the following year.

While the federal plan is no pipedream, its goals can't be achieved without significantly greater investment. This must come from private giving since, due to budgetary pressures, no new federal appropriations are likely anytime soon. For much of President Obama's first term, spending to combat homelessness was robust due to the additional $1.5 billion included in the American Recovery and Reinvestment Act of 2009. But, with that money having dried up and states being too financially strapped, help from people like *you* is critical for ending chronic homelessness. Supporting the types of nonprofits profiled in this chapter offers a major opportunity to make a difference in the lives of people who do not currently have a place to call home. [13]

These investments are crucial given the rise in housing unaffordability during the economic downturn we've been experiencing since 2007. A 2012 report by the National Low-income Housing Coalition reveals some startling trends. One in four renters earns less than 30 percent of the median income for the region where they live, and 76 percent of these extremely low-income renters spend over half their earnings on housing. A person who earns the federal minimum wage ($7.25/hour) needs to work 85 hours a week to afford not having to pay more than 30 percent of earnings for a decent one-bedroom apartment, and must work 101 hours for a two-bedroom apartment.

At the same time that earnings have stagnated, the supply of affordable housing units for low-wage workers has plummeted. For every 100 low-income renters looking for housing, there are only 30 such apartments available. Some of this stock has fallen into disrepair while other units have been rehabbed to serve higher-income tenants. And of course, a significant drop in affordable housing leads to low-income people experiencing a greater susceptibility to becoming homeless. [14]

The good news is that a solution is within reach. The stories recounted in this chapter of individuals who had been down on their luck yet now live better lives in their own homes indicate the worthiness of investing in ending chronic homelessness. Research substantiates the dramatic quality of life changes associated with moving into permanent housing. Two years after chronically homeless people in Denver were moved into their own place, 77 percent remained there. Half had improved physical health and 43 percent improved mental health. Fifteen percent had decreased their substance abuse. Other studies conducted around the U.S. have produced similar findings. Data indicate, moreover, that over the long term the combined cost of providing permanent housing and social services is significantly lower than what we currently spend on medical expenses, temporary shelter, and incarceration. Moving people into their own home *saves* an average of $9,423 a year per capita in the long run (see graph). [15]

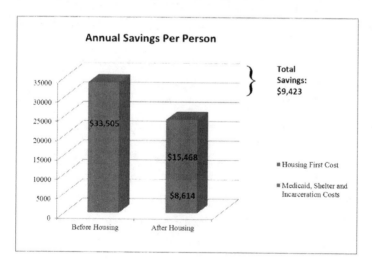

Dane, Frankie, Cheryl, and Peter are each emblems of this success. Their stories illustrate why home is much more than a place to live. For them, having a place of their own fundamentally changed their outlooks on what was possible and attainable in life. Home is a critical anchor for carving out other types of fulfillment, a place to return each day that is one's own and that fuels an array of other opportunities. It's no wonder having a home is often seen as synonymous with the American dream.

Moving into permanent housing enabled Frankie and Cheryl to embark on a path toward gainful employment. For Dane, after years of addiction, having his own place fueled a reconnection with his greatest love: playing music. Peter's passion was art. Once home again, he could enjoy the fruits of his labor and share with his neighbors the sense of worth that creativity offered him. For these four individuals, as for each of us, home is where the heart is.

# 5

## Developing Young Talent

Twenty-two year old Aquila plans to start a catering business in the next few years, a goal that may seem grandiose for someone her age. But, it's actually well within reach given the path her life has taken. She has lots of restaurant kitchen experience, knows several prominent chefs, and is a college graduate.

Six years ago as a high school sophomore, all of this would have seemed impossible. Aquila had a 1.7 GPA in the Baking & Pastry program at a vocational high school in Roxbury, a low-income Boston neighborhood, and had little motivation or direction. She believed she was smart yet didn't have an interest in school, let alone in going to college since most of the people she knew who had done so dropped out and became saddled with debt.

But, Aquila had a passion for cooking – that was clear to anyone who knew her. Chef Lucas, her 10th grade culinary arts teacher, believed she had the ability to cultivate this passion into valuable job skills; all she needed was the determination. So, he pushed her to work hard and encouraged her to think about where her skills could take her. He also introduced her to Toni Elka, who had recently founded Future Chefs in an effort to help youngsters like Aquila.

Toni had been making connections with chefs at Boston-area restaurants. Her vision was that with the right support and encouragement, these could be the sorts of places where someone like Aquila could find gainful employment. And that's just what happened. During summers while she was a student at Southern New Hampshire University, Aquila worked in three different restaurants. When I interviewed her after her junior year, she was working as a line cook at the luxurious Seaport Hotel overlooking Boston Harbor – a job she never would have gotten without the connections she forged through Future Chefs.

*Aquila*

Enabling young people to develop their culinary skills and get job leads are just a part of what this innovative nonprofit does. "Because of Future Chefs, I feel like I am definitely going to be more successful in my life since I have gotten experiences that I couldn't have had otherwise," Aquila told me. She was referring not only to her glowing resume but also to how her involvement with the organization has exposed her to people who have nurtured her self-confidence.

At the Future Chefs cook-off competition after her senior year in high school, her plate received affirmation from renowned Boston chef Chris Douglass. This gave her the conviction that she was cut out to be a chef in a reputable restaurant. That evening Douglass and others who have achieved success in the restaurant industry shared stories about their own career trajectories. Some had undergraduate and/or culinary degrees, some graduated from high school but had not gone to college, and others never even finished high school. Aquila recalls the event as a pivotal moment in her budding motivation to do something significant with her life.

Through her involvement with Future Chefs, Aquila developed career goals and discovered the value of education in achieving them. At Southern New Hampshire University, she further honed her cooking skills. And moving out of state was life-changing since this entailed leaving the poor, mostly black neighborhood where she'd spent her entire life to that point. She met new kinds of people, began to look at her place in the world differently, and grew personally. So much for the girl who didn't want to go to college!

Becoming connected to Future Chefs changed Aquila's life in dramatic ways, giving her mentorship and bolstering her self-confidence. Her mother and grandmother, with whom she lived while growing up, didn't know how to help her develop life goals – even though they certainly cared for and loved her very much. Tragically only a handful of low-income youth in the United States get the type of second chance Future Chefs gave Aquila. Most of the kids she grew up with still lack direction and are either working in dead-end jobs or are unemployed. Few aspire to get post-secondary training. Those who are trying to get ahead lack the adult support to help them do so.

"There are a couple of people who actually, you know, they have had strong people behind them to help them push on but I can count them – I don't even need a whole hand to count those people that I know that are doing something good." As she sees it, kids from her neighborhood are more focused on partying than on trying to move their lives forward.

It's no coincidence that the one friendship Aquila has maintained from high school is with another woman, Shaq, who also went through Future Chefs' program. The two of them were college roommates and plan to open the catering business together. In the meantime, Aquila has returned to Future Chefs as a culinary skills assistant. She is giving back to the program, helping youth with the same sorts of needs she had when she was in high school. [1]

A CLICHÉ WHICH is all too true is that growing up is hard. Kids who have material comforts, live in safe neighborhoods, attend good schools, and get consistent adult guidance have a hard enough time finding their way in the world. Even though most of these kids go to college, a bachelor's degree is no longer a guaranteed launching pad for landing a good job and becoming self-sufficient.

For those kids who grow up lacking family, school, and community supports, the challenges to making a successful transition to adulthood are considerably more formidable. Many have neither a concrete plan for what their lives will be like after high school nor a sense that they even need a plan. While they may have dreams, they lack the strong adult contacts that are so crucial for making those dreams a reality. Unlike their financially better off peers, low-income youth do not have a cushion to lean on while they figure out what they want to do with their lives.

For youth lacking supportive adult role models, becoming connected to an organization like Future Chefs offers a second chance to move their lives forward. Forging relationships with accomplished adults who are interested in youngsters' personal and occupational success enables these kids to chart constructive alternatives to lives that may include menial work, bouts of joblessness, the temptation to abuse drugs, and crime. These organizations function as surrogate extended families, providing guidance, support, and affirmation so that youth can become adults who have both marketable job skills and a positive sense of self-worth.

Future Chefs and the two other nonprofits chronicled in this chapter are on the frontlines addressing a major challenge facing the U.S. economy: people who do not acquire post-secondary skills have little chance of finding decent-paying work. The value of a high school diploma has plummeted over the past few decades, as millions of manufacturing jobs have gone overseas and been replaced by low-wage positions in the service sector. Working at one of these dead-end jobs is actually the lesser of two evils since the alternative is not having a job at all.

Yet, encouraging everyone to go to college is hardly a magic bullet for closing the divide between those who have the skills to secure decent-paying jobs with mobility prospects and those who don't. This is because low-income youth are particularly susceptible to dropping out. A major reason is that college is often unaffordable, even with financial aid. Moreover, many of these kids are not adequately prepared either academically or emotionally, and lack confidence in their ability to succeed.

For 11 years I have taught sociology at a state university that has benefited from the growing popularity of higher education. Whereas 34 percent of 18-24 year olds were enrolled in either a two- or four-year college in 1995, that figure had jumped to nearly 40 percent by 2008. Among the 30-35 students in my introductory-level classes, typically two or three are either not ready or ill-suited to do college-level work. Yet, they may still have talents which, with the right post-secondary training, could be honed into marketable job skills. Most young people do. It's just that the kinds of learning liberal arts professors encourage do not tap these sorts of talents. I have often wondered whether the kids who struggle in my courses might be better off if they cultivated their interests in some other setting. [2]

A 2011 report by the Harvard Graduate School of Education substantiates this long-held intuition of mine. This report is critical of our educational system's narrow focus on academic credentials aimed at preparing youth for a single pathway to success – college. The authors are part of a growing movement of policymakers, activists, and scholars who question the notion of "college for all," seeing it as an oversold and overpriced bill of goods that does not match contemporary economic realities.

Some believe we are in the midst of an education bubble and that like the mid-2000s housing bubble, it too will burst. This means we'll need new models for helping young people transition to adulthood. Besides college, these might include vocational education, apprenticeships, and individualized career counseling. Expanding the array of post-secondary options hinges on the availability of work-based internships that provide solid mentorship, which clearly serves employers' interest in having a skilled workforce.

The Harvard report draws on forecasts by the Center on Education and the Workforce at Georgetown University indicating that about half of all job openings in the coming years will be in positions such as dental hygienist, construction manager, electrician, health technologist, paralegal, and nurse. These require specialized post-secondary training other than a bachelor's degree – such as a certificate, apprenticeship, industry-based certification, employer-based training, or associate degree. A 2012 report by the Georgetown center indicates that one in five jobs in the U.S. – some 29 million jobs in all – pay over $35,000 and require some kind of post-secondary training other than a four-year degree. These jobs are expected to grow *faster* than the subset of the U.S. population that is currently qualified to fill them. [3]

Given these trends, more young people should be encouraged to pursue the post-secondary paths necessary for acquiring the hard skills to fill such positions. And in our service-based economy where it is crucial to come across well to customers, young people also need to learn soft skills. In addition to customer service, these include how to interact with coworkers and supervisors; how to work in teams; how to write an email or letter that sounds professional; the importance of making eye contact; how to dress; and what sorts of conversations topics are appropriate in different situations.

To someone who is middle-class, these may seem like the sorts of skills everybody acquires growing up. Yet, kids in low-income families often do not learn them. Research indicates that the barriers for low-income African Americans who lack soft skills are particularly high since employers may not want to hire them due to longstanding stereotypes about blacks' lack of trustworthiness and dependability on the job. [4]

Fortunately, there is a proven way to elevate the skills of low-income youth and prepare them for good jobs: workforce development. On the surface, this may appear no different from job training programs that have existed for years. But workforce development does much more, teaching the hard skills necessary for specific jobs as well as the soft skills that are so crucial across occupations. Workforce development also helps individuals to access vital social services for overcoming individual barriers to employment – such as childcare, substance abuse counseling, housing, and transportation. Research indicates the most effective workforce development programs train people for positions in a specific, high-demand industry while tailoring the training so that individuals who have repeatedly experienced failure in school, at work, or in their personal lives can learn to believe in their own potential for success. [5]

THERE'S NO WORSE time in recent memory to have started a nonprofit than 2008. This was the height of the Great Recession. Unemployment had hit double digits and the foreclosure crisis was worsening each day. Nonprofits were having a terrible time raising funds. Total charitable contributions in the United States tell 7 percent between 2007 and 2008, one of the largest yearly declines in decades. But this was not going to stand in the way of Future Chefs founder Toni Elka. In 2011 Root Cause showcased this nonprofit as one of its five social innovators that year because of its strong capacity to make an ongoing positive impact on young people.

Not even the worst economic downturn since

the Great Depression could have stopped Toni from pursuing her dream. She had had many years of experience in the restaurant industry as well as a longstanding commitment to working with youth who do not have a lot of adult support or guidance in their lives. The inspiration for creating a nonprofit to help these youth successfully transition to adulthood had been germinating in Toni's head since she was an adolescent. Founding Future Chefs reflects the difficult path her own life had taken, a story all too common in American society. [6]

Originally from a small town in Connecticut, Toni is the oldest of five children and the only one to earn a high school diploma. Her parents were both smart and creative but neither of them went to college. They loved their children yet didn't provide much guidance about where they should go with their lives or how to get there. Toni worked in a variety of dead-end jobs after high school and everywhere she looked, all she saw was evidence of her peers leading dysfunctional lives. Some had gotten pregnant while others, including her boyfriend, were abusing drugs. She knew deep down that she had to get away, so just before she turned 21 she hitchhiked to Boston and showed up at the doorstep of someone she barely knew, asking if she could crash there until she figured out her next move.

Her life slowly began to change when she got in with a crowd of community organizers. Toni felt at home hearing about their work around tenants' rights and other social justice issues, and took notice that these were educated people who had direction. She started taking college classes and found many of them fascinating. Yet, she lacked guidance about where to go with her schooling. This was something she was eventually able to figure out largely on her own, and when she was in her mid-30s she finally finished college. To this day she keenly recognizes how easily her life could have gone down a different path. She was lucky to avoid many of the bad outcomes that others in her situation experience, and wonders what she might have accomplished earlier in life if she hadn't lost so much time finding her way forward.

Her coming-of-age experiences taught Toni two lessons that guide Future Chefs' work: 1) Children rarely grow up to become successful adults without strong adult support; and 2) Youth need opportunities to develop their interests and cultivate them into marketable skills that can enable them to earn a decent living. This might mean the opportunity to do an apprenticeship, earn a certificate, get an associate degree, or a four-year bachelor's degree. "If you don't work intensively with young people and get to know them, then you don't understand what they need and you can't help them move forward," Toni told me in an interview. "You can't help them look at where their strengths and where their challenges are and what they really need to work on."

Although these two lessons hold true for any young person, they're especially vital for the low-income youth with whom Future Chefs primarily works. Many lack adult role models who can help them develop a tangible plan for their lives after high school. What continually inspires Toni is how often she sees herself in these youngsters. She wants to do everything she can to enable them to achieve the successful adulthood that came to her largely by happenstance. "What I'm trying to do here is create a model for working with kids who are like I was – kids who are in high school and have no plan for what is going to happen when they walk out those doors, and no idea about options and choices that have more nuance than just 'going to college.'" [7]

Providing mentorship to low-income youth who display an interest in and aptitude for cooking makes good economic sense. The demand for skilled workers in the food-service industry is high and there are ample opportunities for entry-level workers to advance their careers. Median annual salaries for chefs and restaurant managers in Boston range from $54,000 to $79,000. Nine percent of all workers in Massachusetts are employed in this industry, which is expected to add 22,000 jobs by 2020. Nationwide, this figure stands at 10 percent, making it the second-largest private sector employer in the U.S. Each new restaurant position contributes to the creation of nearly another full-time job elsewhere in the economy. [8]

THE TEENS FUTURE Chefs mentors are culinary arts students at Boston-area vocational schools. They are either recommended by their teachers or find out about the organization through their network of peers at school. Those accepted into the program make a commitment to formulate a plan for successfully moving their lives forward. Toni differentiates Future

Chefs from the many other nonprofits that work with at-risk youth: "We are not a hit-and-run program for kids. We don't just work with them in high school and we don't just work with them after they're already in trouble. We're working with them to put them on a pathway and stick with them until they figure out what the basic rules of success are."

Students become connected with Future Chefs in either 10th or 11th grade and go through a three-phase program. In the first phase, they explore the industry by forging relationships with chefs at local restaurants who mentor them on honing the skills needed for kitchen work and on being committed to the principles of responsibility, discipline, and honesty. The program stresses the importance of positive peer relationships at this time when teens derive much of their motivation from one another.

In phase 2, as high school seniors, students work with Future Chefs staff to develop a specific, individualized plan for their next move after graduation – either post-secondary training in the culinary arts or full-time employment. Students refine their kitchen skills via job shadowing and internships, and also work on developing soft skills like showing up on time, being part of a team, and managing emotions.

After high school graduation they enter phase 3. Here they continue to receive coaching as they begin college or work in the industry. Not only are they now starting to implement their individualized plan, they are also proving their commitment to the success of other disadvantaged youth by serving as mentors for students in phase 1. This way, the program passes on the wealth it creates. The picture below, developed in 2011 when Future Chefs was a Root Cause Social Innovator, depicts the cumulative mission of these three phases. 9

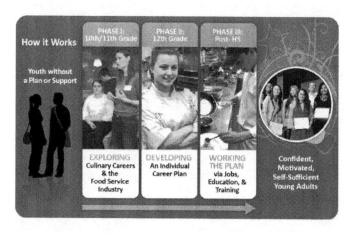

Future Chefs is one of many nonprofits around the U.S. that is effectively implementing workforce development programs. Another exciting organization carrying out such programs in nine U.S. cities is Year Up, which was one of the social innovators Root Cause showcased in 2003. Year Up mentors 18-24-year-old high school graduates who are neither employed nor in college but who have an interest in business and an expressed motivation to succeed.

Recruits spend the first six months taking classes taught by Year Up instructors. These provide opportunities for group interaction and individualized learning. Some of the coursework is designed to build hard skills in either technical or financial areas. These classes include Software Installation, Investment Operation, Fund Accounting, Operating Systems, and

Microsoft Office and Outlook. Other classes like Workplace Norms, Communicating Clearly and Effectively, Working in Teams, and Time Management teach soft skills. While students are taking Year Up courses, they are also enrolled in college. During these six months, they earn a stipend.

Students begin the program with 200 points and receive additional points for favorable performance reviews. They lose points for things like missing meetings, texting in class, or dressing inappropriately. A student whose point total drops to zero is out of the program. Those who successfully complete the coursework can earn up to 18 college credits. They then spend the next six months interning at a financial services firm. Among the extensive list of companies that provide internships are Bank of America, Fidelity, Microsoft, JP Morgan Chase, John Hancock, State Street Bank, and American Express. [10]

Like Toni Elka's connection to Future Chefs, Gerald Chertavian's impetus for founding Year Up was rooted in formative life experiences. He had just graduated from Bowdoin College in the spring of 1987 and was living on Manhattan's Lower East Side. In addition to his high-powered Wall Street job, he volunteered as a Big Brother to a 10-year-old boy named David Heredia. Gerald spent most Saturdays over the next three years with David, who lived with his mother in a small apartment located in a high-crime neighborhood. Gerald also got to know other individuals in David's life – his siblings, cousins, and friends – and noticed that these were people who were smart and talented. Yet, he knew that becoming a successful adult would be a difficult road for them since they were poor and attended the New York City public schools. This meant they lacked the resources and guidance necessary to succeed.

What stuck with Gerald from that experience was a determination someday to help other low-income young people so that, unlike David and others in his neighborhood, they would get the chance to surmount obstacles in their lives. He succinctly characterized Year Up's mission by saying that the organization "does not accept the opportunity gap that exists in our nation. We are determined to provide our urban young adults with the education, guidance, and support they need to realize their potential." [11]

Another exciting nonprofit doing workforce development in the Boston area is More Than Words, which specifically helps foster care youth. Each year roughly 750 kids in Massachusetts and 25,000 nationally age out of the system. The majority of them end up unemployed or underemployed. On top of the challenges most low-income youth face, those in the foster care system are particularly likely to have a learning disability or suffer from mental illness. And a telling indicator of the frequent interruptions they experience in their education is that over 60 percent have neither a high school diploma nor a GED. [12]

A casual visitor to More Than Words' space in Waltham, Mass. is likely to see it as a homey bookstore where one can sit comfortably and read while sipping a tasty drink. And indeed it is. Occasionally, there are author book signings and on the third Friday night of each month there is an open-mic poetry slam. Yet, the store's name highlights a much broader purpose. More Than Words integrates foster care kids into the day-to-day running of a small business. The goal is to redress the fact that throughout their lives these kids have received inconsistent adult support and consequently have low self-esteem. Applicants are referred to the organization by their school counselor, social worker, or probation officer. Experienced participants interview applicants to decide which ones are good fits.

Working at the store becomes the starting point for these kids on their journey to begin taking charge of their lives. They acquire hard skills like knowing how to use different computer applications and doing store inventory, as well as soft skills like how to relate to customers, speak in front of an audience, and send professional emails. And job training is just a piece of More Than Words' mission. Like Future Chefs and Year Up, its broader aim is to help disadvantaged youth successfully transition to adulthood. "While we're teaching them all of these employability skills, what we're really doing is giving them the sense that they matter – that they're part of something," said executive director Jodi Rosenbaum. "The fundamental piece of what helps young people make change in their lives is that they actually realize they're worth it, that they're part of something, that people care about them, and that they're smart enough and capable enough to live and love their lives." [13]

Workers at More Than Words hold two complementary jobs. Their business job involves working 20-30 hours a week as part of a team that handles all aspects of running the store. This includes tracking financial information, doing publicity, planning and hosting author events and open-mic nights, running weekly team meetings, and training new workers. In their "me" job, the goal is self-advancement. They work to overcome barriers in their lives that are preventing them from taking full advantage of the valuable skills they are gaining in their business job. They are each assigned a case manager who assists them with such things as getting a bank account or personal ID card, helping them get back into school or stay in school, counseling them about the types of work they might want to do after leaving the program, and informing them of job leads.

Each month More Than Words participants set personal goals for which they are held accountable. Performance reviews and promotions are based as much on meeting these goals as on their work in the bookstore. During the 6-12 months that people hold these two jobs, they also work to craft a plan for what lies ahead next in their lives. The organization provides at least another year of case management to ensure that program participants can move on, either to another job or to college.

"MY LIFE BEFORE More Than Words was hectic," says Brian. "I was in New Bedford involved in street, drug, and crime activity; that's the only business I really knew, selling drugs on the street corner. It was the wrong activity that no 12- or 13-year-old should ever be involved in. More Than Words opened my eyes to what

I wanted to do in life and helped me set that path and lead my way to the future. I didn't have much self-confidence, and my communication skills weren't all there. I didn't believe in myself much, and More Than Words was always there by my side and pushing me along when I wanted to stop. " [14]

*Brian*

There are many other success stories. Consider Rebecca, who came to her interview feeling uncomfortable speaking openly about her troubled past. She was accepted into the program but withdrew after a month because she wasn't ready to meet the high expectations she needed to set for herself. When she reapplied and reentered the program, she was ready. She learned to be excited about her work, whether that was a book a customer was interested in or a latte she was serving when she worked as a barista in the café. She also became enthusiastic about her own growth. More Than Words inspired her to want to continue her education, and she's now in college. She no longer feels victimized by her past but instead is in control of where her life is going. [15]

*Rebecca*

Bryan H. is a support technician at Perot Systems. He's confident this job will enable him to improve his skills and further his career – an outlook he didn't always have about himself. He attributes this transformation to Year Up, which helped him overcome his fear of public speaking and showed him how to communicate ideas effectively. This high school dropout who earned his GED aspires someday to manage his own IT team.

*Bryan H.*

"When my parents were having problems and getting divorced, I was about 16 or 17 and feeling really bad," said Aly. "It was something that really affected me and when Future Chefs came into my life, it was like 'oh, you are really good.' This was something that I couldn't see. I knew that culinary was easy to me because I knew what to do because my mom had taught me, but that was it. I couldn't see what that meant. I knew I could use a knife but that was it. And then when they came into my life they were like, 'oh you're good at cooking – you could do this, you could do that. You can get a good job or get into college.'" [16]

*Aly*

One might wonder how much individual success stories like these truly reveal about the overall effectiveness of a nonprofit's work. Future Chefs' Toni Elka addressed this issue with regard to Aquila, the woman whose dramatic tale opened this chapter.

"Tell me how someone who graduates from Madison Park High School with a 1.7 GPA and doesn't want to go to college is going to move forward. You tell me nobody in your family has gone to college, you live in Dudley Station, you like cooking and you're leaving high school and you've never been to a fancy restaurant in the city. You've probably never even stayed at a hotel, and you want to get a job at one. How would you end up in an internship at the Seaport Hotel three years later? You wouldn't. You would not know Jodie Adams, Chris Douglass, or Rachel Klein (prominent Boston chefs)."

Such success stories illustrate that workforce development programs can be instrumental in helping disadvantaged youth carve out a path to a successful future. These stories underscore the need for interventions during the teenage years, which isn't too late to make a profound difference in a person's life.

In addition to tales of personal transformation, there are other indicators that the nonprofits chronicled in this chapter are making a significant impact. Ninety percent of those in either phase 2 or 3 of Future Chefs' program are in an internship or job that is building their resume in the culinary arts. And of those who have completed phase 3, 90 percent are enrolled in or have already completed post-secondary training. Almost half of Year Up grads are in college and 87 percent work at jobs with average starting salaries of $15 an hour, or $30,000 a year. A 2011 study by the Economic Mobility Corporation documented that in the year after they participated in Year Up, people earned 30 percent more than those who'd applied to the program but did not participate. [17]

Eighty-two percent of the youth who work at More Than Words have attained or are on course to get their GEDs, compared to 50 percent of all foster care youth. Whereas 75 percent of these youth are unemployed or underemployed, the same percentage of More Than Words participants works full-time or attends college. Ninety percent of participants have improved their self-efficacy, which the organization tracks based on goal setting, effort, persistence, and recovery from setbacks.

Executive Director Jodi Rosenbaum explained the simple reason why. "Work is an incredibly rehabilitative and restorative thing. To get up and have something purposeful to do, to get up where you have things that you're immediately able to meet with success. I think that is a fundamental piece of the model. If you look at research on resilience, there's a whole field just on skill acquisition. When you learn to do things, your whole self-confidence changes and so by design they meet with success when they start here and it might be little successes like learning how to sort fiction from non-fiction or learning how to use a scanner gun and scan books. And there's something really empowering about making money and running a business, especially for many of our kids to see that they have the capacity to legitimately make money." [18]

A BEDROCK AMERICAN value is that those who are motivated to get ahead will do so. Such determination, of course, hinges on a person believing s/he is deserving of a better life. Families that struggle to make ends meet tend to be places where there's a dearth of strong adult support to nurture kids' aspirations. This isn't because parents don't care about their kids. Parents may well want a better future for their children, yet if they themselves have had little formal schooling and limited employment opportunities they likely don't know how to guide their kids toward success. Consequently, low-income parents often lack confidence in their ability to help their kids believe in themselves.

Jay MacLeod, who spent 25 years studying the lives of a group of low-income men in the Boston area, learned upon meeting them as teens in the mid-1980s that they had a dire view of what the future held in store for them. When he asked where they saw themselves in 20 years, most said either unemployed, in jail, or dead. He came to see that their bleak hopes oddly enough made sense given that their parents, who had grown up poor with limited education and erratic work histories, couldn't provide them with much guidance about how to achieve future success. However, with interventions aimed at cultivating both occupational and life success youth who have grown up in circumstances like the ones MacLeod chronicled can turn their lives around. [19]

"I didn't have any support in my life and it was hard," says 19-year-old Zuleimy, reflecting on the period before she joined Future Chefs two years earlier. "It is really hard – you feel like you don't want anything for yourself because nobody else wants it for you. My sister dropped out of school so everyone in my family expected me to go down that same path. But when I met Toni and Ann (Future Chefs staff), they told me that is not going to happen. It's only going to happen if you let it happen." Whereas a lack of family support had caused Zuleimy to become apathetic about school, she was now surrounded by adults helping her to believe in herself and to care about doing well in school while holding down a job and volunteering with Future Chefs. In becoming connected to the organization, she had started to see the value that education could have in enabling her to succeed and was willing to undergo the sacrifices necessary to make that a reality. Sherley, a Year Up grad who works at Bank of America, similarly expressed how the program "made me realize that everything is possible – that once I set a goal for myself, I can achieve it." [20]

*Zuleimy*                               *Sherley*

In America, everything indeed is possible *if* a person can get the consistent support and guidance needed to fuel and reinforce that sentiment. Nonprofits like Future Chefs, Year Up, and More Than Words make this belief come true for kids who have few, if any, concrete plans for achieving a brighter future – kids on a path for dead-end jobs as well as possibly bouts of unemployment, drug abuse, and crime. These nonprofits not only teach youth marketable skills but, more importantly, nurture their self-confidence. Even though the disadvantages people have experienced over the course of their lives cannot magically be erased, the promising work of these organizations demonstrates that low-income youth do not face insurmountable hurdles. For this reason alone, they deserve second chances.

A WIDE ARRAY of industries is ripe for workforce development programs. With sufficient financial backing this model could be extended into trades such as landscaping, building renovation, historic preservation, and auto repair. "There should be Future Childcare Workers and Future Nurses and Future Builders," commented Future Chefs' Toni Elka. "Structured pathways should be created so that there are clear steps indicating this is what you do. But they should also be focused on the transition from adolescence to adulthood so that young people aren't just getting the technical skills that they need but they're getting the soft skills and the life skills and the connection to the adult community."

Yet federal spending on workforce development has met the hatchet in recent years, falling from $1.6 billion in 1994 to $900 million in 2010. A major reason for these cuts is the lack of significant results stemming from too much emphasis being placed on rapid job placement. This prevents people from getting the chance to develop skills that can be transferable to other work settings. Moreover, programs that do not include intensive, ongoing mentoring leave participants without the self-confidence to sustain them as they progress throughout their adult lives. [21]

President Obama's orientation has certainly been on the right track. In February 2009, he outlined before a joint session of Congress an agenda for putting more resources into pathways other than college to prepare disadvantaged young people for decent-paying jobs. That June, he visited the Washington office of Year Up and praised the organization for providing such a pathway. The following month, he announced a $12 billion initiative to boost community colleges – a plan not implemented until early 2011 and funded at just $2 billion. In June 2011 he proposed an expansion of this program. Yet, the future of this agenda remains uncertain given the strong mandate in Washington to cut spending. Budgetary constraints make it unlikely the government will act to expand funding for workforce development anytime soon. Therefore, it is incumbent upon us as private citizens to provide additional support. [22]

Given that we're a nation which trumpets opportunity for all, investing in workforce development is a way to put our money where our mouths are. Such an investment reflects our commitment to the principle that every young person deserves the chance to develop his or her potential and lead a successful life. But, supporting workforce development programs is not simply a matter of social justice. It also reflects the longstanding value we place on helping the "deserving" poor. Those who participate in these programs have voluntarily chosen to seek guidance about how to move their lives forward. Being accepted into the programs run by More Than Words, Year Up, and Future Chefs is not easy, and succeeding in them is even harder. But for the youth who participate, that is part of the attraction. This is often the first time in their lives they have been held accountable to high standards set by people who care about them and whom they respect.

Not offering this type of second chance is a missed opportunity that carries serious societal consequences. "Having so many disconnected young people in America is in and of itself unacceptable for those young adults. But, it also doesn't help our country produce the skilled workforce that we need to be globally competitive," commented Year Up founder and CEO Gerald Chertavian. By inadequately preparing so many youth for today's economy, we are allowing lots of talent to go untapped. Isn't talent a precious resource that we should be cultivating and nurturing, not wasting?

As I write these words, U.S. unemployment hovers around eight percent and yet many employers are unhappy with the labor pool available to them. A recent survey of several hundred firms revealed considerable dissatisfaction with the low skill set and lack of professionalism of many high school graduates nowadays. These concerns will only grow as we come out of the economic downturn. It's no wonder, then, why companies are so eager to invest in workforce development programs. Year Up's Senior Director of Development, Michael Goldstein, indicated that 64 percent of the program's funding comes from sponsoring companies. Because they are involved in designing the program's curriculum, courses align with employer needs, thereby producing a pipeline for hiring skilled workers. [23]

Enabling young people to acquire valuable job skills and become emotionally prepared to lead successful adult lives is a smart investment when we consider the massive costs it would reduce. Youth unemployment is more than double the rate across the entire population and joblessness is particularly high among Black and Latino youth. Unemployment is highly correlated with crime, and especially for those under 25. Crime not only diminishes the quality of life and raises public fears of victimization but also costs taxpayers billions of dollars a year.

A report by the New York City Center for Economic Opportunity calculates the substantial returns accrued from investing in workforce development programs. After tallying increases in workers' earnings and tax contributions along with reductions in welfare expenditures and unemployment insurance payments, the study found that these programs can yield over nine dollars for every dollar spent. And this doesn't even take into account increases in employer output or savings from lowered incarceration expenses. Thus, it is clear we have before us an incredible investment opportunity that can yield substantial societal benefit. [24]

# 6

# Getting the Right Start

The future wouldn't be as bright for two-year old Carnell if it weren't for Vickie. His parents, Antoinette and Carles, met her several months before he was born. It was supposed to be one of the most exciting times in their lives – given the anticipation surrounding the birth of their first child – yet it felt like one of the scariest. Antoinette was only 18, having just graduated from high school. She and Carles needed help yet didn't know where to turn.

A certain amount of anxiety is to be expected among first-time parents. This is, after all, a huge life change for which no one can fully prepare. However, the anxiety can be particularly acute for people facing the types of stresses familiar to Antoinette and Carles. Fortunately, they learned about Nurse-Family Partnership. This nonprofit with sites around the United States provides assistance to new parents experiencing significant financial strain in their lives. People are assigned to a nurse, who offers various kinds of support until the baby turns two, meeting every week or two in the mother's home. This direct and ongoing contact with a knowledgeable and skilled professional enables program participants to take on the role of parent more capably and give their child as many opportunities as possible to thrive.

When they met Vickie, Antoinette and Carles were each experiencing considerable hardship. Antoinette lived with her mother in low-income housing and money was perpetually tight. She had been unemployed for some time. When she finally landed a temp job, she soon had to give it up because she was having severe asthma attacks. Carles had his own issues to work through, which became exacerbated when he learned he was going to become a dad. He worried about how he could sufficiently be there for his child given his own family background. He was one of 20 children, his father having been absent for much of his life and his mother having been a long-time drug addict. She was once so desperate for a fix that she sold his only pair of jeans to buy drugs.

From the moment Vickie met the expectant couple she was an unwavering source of support, helping them in many ways to prepare for their new life. When they were incurring mounting repair bills because of car troubles, she went with them to find another car. She also accompanied them to the Medicaid office to straighten out a problem with their health coverage. Sometimes, she arranged to meet with them in a public place so Carles could get free internet access to look for jobs. And with the small allowance from Nurse-Family Partnership that she had at her disposal, Vickie brought him a new pair of jeans.

After Antoinette gave birth, the conversations with Vickie shifted to good parenting skills. Topics not only involved basics like how to hold, feed, and diaper a baby but also how to meet the challenging emotional hurdles of parenthood. So when Carles confessed to Vickie that he felt jealous because Carnell was bonding with Antoinette but not with him, Vickie indicated that this would change. "Be patient," she reassured him. "The more you play with Carnell and interact with him, the more he'll get used to you."

At the time they graduated from the Nurse-Family Partnership program, Antoinette and Carles each had a job and they both had their sights set on going to college. They were also in the thick of planning their wedding. These positive life changes boded well for Carnell, who was in daycare and thriving. They pointed to the likelihood that his parents would continue to be able to meet his developmental needs. Unlike so many other low-income children, he would be prepared to start kindergarten when he turned five.

A couple of years earlier – when Antoinette found out she was pregnant – the odds had been much greater that Carnell would become just another poster child of the academic achievement gap. But, with Vickie's support and encouragement there was now much less of a chance that this would happen. It seemed likelier that he was on the road to achieving success in life.

Each year Nurse-Family Partnership helps 25,000 babies and their parents successfully navigate this time of transition so that they may feel excited about the momentous change taking place in their lives. The organization has produced significant results. Expectant mothers maintain greater contact with the baby's father, the child has fewer language delays, and is less frequently involved in the criminal justice system while growing up. Moreover, these partnerships between nurses and new parents save the government money that would otherwise go toward incarceration, special education, and other social services. This amounts to over $27,000 by the time the child turns 12, with additional savings thereafter. [1]

EVEN THOUGH EVERYBODY benefits when a child starts off life on the right foot, thrives academically, and becomes a productive member of society, stories like Carnell's can be a tough sell for donors. Since these kids are on a path with encouraging signs that they will not drop out of school and not be prone to commit crime, their likely future successes just don't seem as heroic as those of the individuals chronicled in the previous two chapters - people who at one time had experienced significant hardship yet now have a new lease on life.

Hearing about how Future Chefs helped Aquila develop career aspirations or how Hearth enabled Peter to move from a shelter into his own home warms our hearts. There is a stark contrast between the positive life paths these individuals are now on and the bleak road they used to travel. Dane spent many years as a homeless junkie but now, through assistance from

HomeStart, has his own apartment and is drug-free. Brian used to abuse drugs yet has been clean for several years. He is working at More Than Words bookstore, where he is acquiring valuable job skills and gaining self-confidence. There's nothing quite like the admiration we reserve for people who beat the odds and overcome significant obstacles in their lives.

It's no wonder, then, that Liz Murray's 2010 memoir *Breaking Night* struck such a chord. It chronicles her life as the daughter of drug-addicted parents, both of whom contracted HIV and subsequently died of AIDS. Though Murray became homeless as a teenager, she stayed focused on education and eventually graduated from Harvard. The made-for-TV movie *Homeless to Harvard* publicized her dramatic life change. Murray's transformation underscores the core challenge in motivating donors to support interventions very early in life so that kids avoid going down the wrong path: there is no "before" story against which to compare a person's successes. Yet, wouldn't it make sense to invest in strategies that *prevent* kids from enduring the hardships that stem from having been born into poverty?

We can draw an analogy from the 2009 federal stimulus implemented soon after Barack Obama became president. The $787 billion spending package drew criticism despite many economists' assessment that it created millions of jobs, enabling the nation to avert prolonged double-digit unemployment and perhaps another Great Depression. Avoiding catastrophe just isn't very noteworthy since it's hard to put a value on human misery that doesn't occur. [2]

Yet, we must not let our emotions inhibit us from embracing sensible strategies for restoring the American dream. It's true that compared to youth or adults who receive help and then turn their lives around, there is relatively little drama surrounding assistance that enables children like Carnell to thrive from as early in life as possible. But that shouldn't be reason to decide not to invest in programs that provide enrichment to ensure that economically disadvantaged kids are prepared to enter kindergarten at age five. The very goal of this enrichment is, after all, to prevent them from experiencing problems later in life. We must not let the absence of drama lessen the importance of investing in kids' futures. As citizens of a nation experiencing a widening opportunity divide, we have a responsibility to do what we know works to mitigate it. There is compelling evidence about the benefits that investing in early childhood education provides both to low-income families and to our society as a whole.

QUINCY COMMUNITY ACTION Programs is one of many nonprofits around the U.S. working to mitigate the glaring inequalities among children that are evident within the first year of life and become pronounced by age two. QCAP is one of 24 agencies in Massachusetts created during the 1960s as part of Lyndon Johnson's war on poverty. It is a soup-to-nuts organization that addresses low-income people's multiple areas of need: jobs, housing, food and nutrition, fuel assistance, and money management. The agency also carries out Head Start, the federal early childhood enrichment program that serves nearly a million pre-school kids per year across all 50 states. It provides early childhood education free of charge to three- and four-year-olds living in poverty.

The goal of Head Start is to compensate for the fact that these kids were born into households that often cannot provide the physical, emotional, and intellectual nurturance those in higher-income households typically get. The program consequently promotes development across multiple areas: cognition (including special education), health (physical, mental, and dental), nutrition, and social services. Head Start families are typically unable to afford to send their children to *any* preschool, let alone one that meets the program's high standards. [3]

When I spoke with QCAP's Head Start Program Director Anne Leister and its Educational Coordinator Keather Reickle, they couldn't say enough about the ways they see children growing daily from the program. "You can go into a classroom at this time of the year (springtime) and you can point to the kids who are ready for kindergarten," claimed Anne. "They have confidence and social skills. They are verbal, they are healthier looking, and they have been eating healthy foods for three years at lunch and at snack. They have a sense of community. I was telling Keather I was in a classroom the other day and the children were all waking up from nap and one of the little boys was slow to wake up and he's got three friends sitting around him, and they're telling me he loves Mickey Mouse. So they have the Mickey Mouse doll on his pillow so that when he opens his eyes, he sees Mickey

Mouse. And one of them was gently rubbing his hands and saying 'Come on, Jimmy, it's time to wake up.' And they're saying 'He likes to sleep a long time, he likes to sleep late.' So I said to Keather, 'What is that saying? It's saying something very good.' And she said it's about a sense of community and emotional health." [4]

Reaching developmental milestones is, of course, a miracle to marvel in *any* child. It is particularly noteworthy for kids served by Head Start given that they were born into families that often experience a range of stresses in addition to being poor. These may include unemployment, mental illness, malnutrition, substance abuse, violence, neglect, and homelessness. Indeed, the very reason this program was created and why it endures is because the needs it serves are massive.

These stresses produce a significant gap in academic achievement among American children based on the environments in which they grow up. A report published by the nonpartisan research center Child Trends documents significant disparities in cognitive development by 24 months of age, some even manifesting themselves within the first year of life. This is noteworthy considering that about half of all children in the U.S. live in families with household incomes less than twice the federal poverty line and nearly a quarter grow up in poverty. [5]

Psychologists Betty Hart and Todd Risley have perhaps best illuminated the early onset of the educational achievement gap. In a groundbreaking study, they spent about an hour each month with families from across the income spectrum, observing how parents used language while interacting with their children. In total they studied 42 families from the time children were seven to nine months old until just after they turned three. The size of kids' vocabularies and the frequency of their verbal utterances mirrored the vast gaps among their parents.

Those who worked in professional jobs had about a 50 percent larger vocabulary than working-class parents, and this same discrepancy showed up among their children. When the researchers returned to study these children as 3rd graders, they found the income-related gaps had grown even larger over time. These data point to how the cognitive advantages or disadvantages kids experience during early childhood create an ongoing trajectory. The brain is most malleable until about age three and becomes dramatically less so after six. The first few years of life are a time when children are ripe for absorbing so many different kinds of information and stimuli. This is also when a child develops lifelong habits and tastes for learning. Experiences during this critical time significantly shape which kinds of new learning opportunities kids will seek out later in life. [6]

HEAD START TEACHERS record data about physical and mental health as well as cognitive development within 45 days after a child enters the program. Teachers then reassess each child three times per year, documenting on a five-point scale proficiency across 13 learning domains. These scores inform decisions about how to target a particular child's areas of strength or need and about whether outside help is needed to meet these goals. At the time children are about to complete the program, on average 85 percent consistently score fours or fives; the rest score mostly in the threes, which is also acceptable for entry into kindergarten. [7]

The strongest data about Head Start's impact come from studies comparing children who participated in high-quality early childhood enrichment programs with those of similar backgrounds who did not. The Head Start Impact Study conducted in the mid-2000s tracked the progress of low-income children who were placed in a Head Start program at either age three or four versus control groups of kids the same age who were allowed to enroll in other early childhood education programs. While it ethically made sense not to deny kids in the control groups a preschool education, the reality is that for a significant percentage of poor children, the alternative to participating in Head Start is no preschool at all. Fewer than 40 percent of poor three-year-olds and fewer than two-thirds of poor four-year-olds attend preschool; for kids from families with annual household incomes exceeding $100,000, these figures are 71 percent and 89 percent respectively. [8]

"On nearly every measure of quality traditionally used in early childhood research," the Head Start Impact Study report concluded, "the Head Start group had more positive experiences than those in the control group." Both Head Start groups attended higher-quality programs, as measured by factors such as teacher credentials, classroom instruction, and teacher-student ratios. Average vocabulary scores were three percentage points higher for three-year-old Head Start participants and four percentage points higher for four-year-old participants than for their respective control groups. [9]

IMPASSIONED ACTIVIST JONATHAN Kozol has devoted his career to documenting the stark inequalities so many kids – particularly Black and Hispanic children – experience in America's public schools. In one school he visited in the South Bronx, on a rainy afternoon a stream of water flowed down the stairwell. Another school built for 1000 students enrolled 1500. At several schools, there were 34 or more kids in a class. Many did not have a gymnasium or a place to play outside. Millions of low-income children attend schools that lack the resources to spur academic achievement on a par with schools serving kids from more privileged backgrounds, let alone the resources to make up for achievement gaps that have become pronounced by the time kids enter kindergarten.

This is because K-12 funding comes from local property taxes, which reflect home values. Kozol documented that the suburban town of Millburn, New Jersey spent about $1500 more each year per student than the fledgling city of East Orange. Whereas Millburn could attract more experienced teachers, East Orange – like other school districts in low-income communities – had to hire people who lacked certification in the subjects they taught. These disparities extend to a school's course offerings, how up-to-date its lab equipment is, and the quantity of the computers, books, and art supplies it can afford. [10]

It's no wonder, then, that the Head Start Impact Study report confirmed something which has become critics' rallying cry: the gains children make fade by the end of first grade, as evidenced by the inconsequential differences in test scores between Head Start kids and their peers. Yet, what else can we expect given that most kids in Head Start go on to attend the sorts of schools Kozol describes?

When I spoke to Chris Sieber, Development Director at Action for Boston Community Development, which runs Head Start programs throughout the city, she emphasized that this fade-out shouldn't be seen as the program's Achilles Heel. "It's a little odd to expect that we can give kids an injection of great education for a few years and expect that it will overcome and eliminate the challenges in their educational lives after that. Public schools are killers for these kids." They were born unequal and after Head Start they go on to attend low-quality schools that exacerbate their disadvantage. [11]

A further reason to de-emphasize the significance of the fade-out effect is that it's based on test scores, which hardly provide a rich picture of the long-term impacts of an enriched early childhood education. During the mid-2000s Harvard economist Raj Chetty and his colleagues collected follow-up data about adults who, as elementary school children, had participated in Project Star. In this experiment conducted in Tennessee during the 1980s, children were randomly assigned to classes of varying sizes for grades K-3. The researchers documented many positive outcomes among those who had been assigned to the smallest classes. Now in their 30s, they were more likely than other study participants to attend college. They also out-earned students in the other classes, including those of similar family backgrounds. The fact that these high achievers had received a top-notch education beginning in kindergarten, the researchers concluded, was decisive in explaining their achievements. Since this study illustrates the long-term effects of different qualities of early childhood educational experiences, its findings would seem to be equally applicable to the preschool years. [12]

The strongest evidence of the gains that enriched early childhood educational programs enable low-income kids to make comes from a study done in Michigan during the mid-1960s. The High/Scopes Perry Preschool randomly assigned 58 low-income children to attend its preschool while 65 other kids of similar backgrounds did not attend preschool at all.

Researchers have followed the two groups over time. The differences between these people, now in their 40s and 50s, are astounding. Those who attended the High/Scopes Perry Preschool are likelier to:

- Have graduated high school (65% v. 45%)
- Be employed (76% v. 62%)
- Own a home (37% v. 28%)
- Have higher earnings (median earnings were $20,800 v. $15,300)

Those who attended High/Scopes Perry Preschool are also much less likely to have been arrested or to have spent time in prison. These data are a powerful illustration of just how much low-income kids – who often experience an array of stresses in addition to material hardships – can thrive when given access to a high-quality preschool. [13]

Another landmark study, conducted in North Carolina during the early 1970s, shows that when this type of opportunity is made available to poor children, they're not the only ones who benefit. The Carolina Abecedarian Project was like the High/Scopes Perry Study in that it compared kids randomly assigned to attend a high-quality preschool with those who didn't attend any preschool at all. Participants have periodically been tracked over time. The most recent data collected at age 21 revealed the preschool participants were more likely to have completed high school, attend a four-year college, and even to have attained higher test scores. Because the children were in a full-time program, their mothers had more time to get training and employment. As a result, they earned on average $3750 more per year over the 21-year period than did mothers of kids in the control group. [14]

Enabling poor children to get a high-quality preschool education has even greater positive effects in terms of what parents can give to their children. Since early childhood is a time when kids are so dependent on caregivers, a crucial aim of Head Start is to enhance parents' capacity to enrich their children's lives. The program strives to compensate for the fact that low-income parents tend to be less involved in their kids' education than higher-income parents. Considerable research has shown how parents at different income levels contribute to gaps in children's cognitive development. There are disparities in how much parents read to their child, how much they reinforce classroom lessons, how much interaction they have with teachers about their child's progress in school, and how often they attend school events. [15]

Annette Lareau, a sociology professor at the University of Pennsylvania, has spent many years documenting the reasons for this disparity. In one study, she observed the families of first graders in two communities in California: one working class and the other upper-middle class. Lareau noticed that the higher-income parents, who were more heavily involved in their children's' education, tended to know one another and keep each other abreast of their kids' progress in school. Whereas the higher-income parents typically held professional jobs that encouraged networking as a way to get ahead, lower-income parents held blue-collar or service-sector jobs which seldom required them to develop these skills.

The two sets of families also differed in their "cultural capital." This is the knowledge, interests, and tastes people accumulate throughout their lives, chiefly from their families but also from their experiences in school, at work, and elsewhere. The higher-income parents Lareau observed had the understanding, which the lower-income parents often lacked, that being continually involved in their children's education would have a significant positive impact on their kids' futures. Having richer cultural capital enabled the higher-income parents to be more skilled at interacting with teachers and socializing with the parents of their kids' classmates. [16]

Given these disparities, one of Head Start's chief aims is to teach parents how to be integrally involved in their children's upbringing. Parents are required to participate in trainings at the preschool, to attend teacher-parent conferences, and to be available to meet with social workers and other specialists who work with their child. Head Start centers provide parents with tips about helping their child become ready to read, reinforcing school curricula, and teaching kids how to behave appropriately in groups. Hence, Head Start's lasting impacts reside both in the skills kids learn at school and in parents' capacity to build upon these skills in the home and community. [17]

AS VALUABLE AS Head Start is for poor families, Action for Boston Community Development's Chris Sieber emphasizes that early childhood enrichment programs are "much more effective if you're reaching babies when they're very young and then following them for several years. Those gains are more sustained the longer you have a kid involved. So if you can be deeply engaged with that family for five years, it makes a much bigger difference than if you're engaged with the family for one year." [18]

This was the thinking in the mid-1990s when the federal government created Early Head Start. It is like the traditional Head Start program that has been in existence since the 1960s in that its focus is on childhood enrichment and parental support. The key difference is that this program often starts while the baby is still in utero. Early Head Start provides comprehensive services to cultivate children's physical, emotional, and cognitive development while also nurturing parents' investment in this development. Until the child is 15 months old, service delivery is done in the home; after that, s/he enters a center-based program that continues until the transition to Head Start at age three. [19]

Kids in Early Head Start benefit in powerful ways. They make greater gains in vocabulary and cognitive development compared to kids from similar backgrounds not enrolled in the program. Children in Early Head Start also exhibit greater attention and engagement with peers. And the program enables parents to have more positive interactions with their kids; they spend greater amounts of time engaged in play, are more likely to read to their children, and less likely to spank them. [20]

Despite the advantages of providing enrichment to poor children as early in life as possible, Early Head Start serves just a fraction of the kids who need it. Whereas 133,878 were in the program during the 2009-10 school year, 983,809 kids participated in Head Start. This gap stems from service providers' chief goal that low-income children achieve "school readiness" by kindergarten. Given that there are limited resources for providing an enriched early childhood education free of charge, the critical time to begin investing in school readiness has traditionally been age three. [21]

Fortunately, many nonprofits around the U.S. are working to mitigate the achievement gap from birth or earlier. One is Nurse-Family Partnership which, as we saw at the opening of this chapter, helped Antoinette, Carles, and their baby Carnell. Other organizations support parents during pregnancy and continue to provide assistance throughout the first years of life. They connect families with Early Head Start and other services such as housing assistance and counseling around substance abuse, domestic violence, and mental health issues. These services promote a developmentally rich childhood.

Another organization that aims to leave no child behind is Room to Grow, which started in New York City and now assists poor children and their families in Boston too. Between the two sites, the organization serves about 700 clients per year. Founder Julie Burns had one goal in mind when she created Room to Grow in 1998: to offer poor families resources so that kids could avoid the array of lifelong disadvantages which otherwise loom on the horizon. Burns had been working as a child & adolescent therapist at a New York City clinic and saw firsthand how often low-income kids' troubles stemmed from the stresses that often accompany growing up poor. [22]

Families become connected with Room to Grow after being referred by prenatal care providers, birthing hospitals, and community health centers. The aim is for families to begin the program by the first few weeks of their newborn's life, and ideally for expectant mothers to become connected to the organization during their final trimester. Parents meet with social workers four times a year until their child turns three. The family is given whatever supplies a child may need including toys, books, bottles, blankets, and clothes.

But, social workers don't just offer free stuff; they also talk about how best to use these things. In giving out bottles, they might initiate a conversation about nutritious eating and the importance of families having meals together. Providing free books may be part of a discussion about ways to engage a child in reading. The point is that since healthy child development during the first three years of life hinges on parental involvement, the program emphasizes childrearing skills. Social workers devise and share strategies for helping parents meet the daily challenges of baby care. [23]

"Room to Grow has made a huge difference in my life. I have become a very calm parent," commented Taniesha Henry, a 24-year-old parent who participated in the program with her baby. "I'm no longer confused. I have lots of confidence." In addition to testimonials from parents, the organization also rigorously evaluates how well it is meeting its goal to build a strong foundation for babies born into poverty so that they will stay on track developmentally with kids from higher-income families. Parents give feedback via surveys and interviews, and kids are followed 6 and 12 months after graduating from the program. An independent consultant also assesses how well the program is reaching its benchmarks. [24]

The evidence from these evaluations is encouraging. Over 80 percent of clients complete the program, a noteworthy figure given the daily struggles and challenges low-income families face. Ninety percent of parents indicated on the 2008 client survey that they had become more knowledgeable about their children's developmental milestones and 88 percent responded that Room to Grow had taught them how to maintain a healthy parent-child relationship. "Inquisitive parenting is something that we really nurture here," commented the Boston office's Executive Director, Saskia Epstein. "We have seen a great deal of change in that area. In some ways, it's quite simple: a parent who doesn't know how to play with their child who begins to understand the importance of play and also is given support and information and guidance and the right tools to be able to get down on the floor and actively play with their child. That kind of transformation is happening at Room to Grow and is a really common and consistent thread in the work that we're doing." [25]

ROOM TO GROW has had unusual fundraising success because high-profile donors have been on board since its inception. Founder Julie Burns is married to renowned documentary filmmaker Ken Burns and the couple's onetime neighbor, actress Uma Thurman, was also an early supporter. However, for most nonprofits that invest in early childhood enrichment their work is a tough sell. Donors rarely consider these charities when making contributions or when deciding where and what types of volunteer opportunities to pursue. The primary fundraising barrier these organizations face is that their work is preventative, and therefore lacks a transformative narrative.

"When you're working with a child from birth to three, the change that we're seeking is not going to be measured pre and post in the way that a high school dropout who then goes to college can be measured and is also quite visible in the impact," commented Room to Grow's Saskia Epstein. "We tend, as a society, to stand around and wait for things to happen and try to fix the situation. When we're trying to fix something and you can see that it's broken first and then fix after, that kind of evidence is far more dramatic and compelling to people in terms of the demonstration of change that we seek to make."

There is strong public support for investing in early childhood education; it's just that this support tends to be for greater government funding. A national poll by Peter D. Hart Research Associates found that 80 percent of those who were knowledgeable about Head Start had a favorable impression of it. A survey by ORC International further revealed that this sentiment transcended party lines. Other data confirm that there's broad public support for expanding government funding for universal preschool. Yet, this seems unlikely to happen in the foreseeable future given the strong political sentiment nowadays for reducing social spending. [26]

The fact that over 90 percent of funding for the roughly 1600 nonprofit Head Start providers around the United States comes from the federal government might suggest there is no need for people like you to support these organizations. Think again. FY2010 Head Start funding was just $7.2 billion, and even the infusion of another $2.1 in federal stimulus money during 2009 and 2010 was insufficient to meet the escalating need. Rising enrollments coupled with stagnant funding have meant a steady reduction in per-pupil expenditures. In Massachusetts alone, an estimated $600 million more a year would be needed to ensure that all poor children in the state have access to a high-quality preschool.

Nonprofits that support Head Start and other programs to offset the academic achievement gap – organizations like Quincy Community Action Programs, Action for Boston Community Development, Nurse-Family Partnership, and Room to Grow – need wider sources of support. Yet, since most of these nonprofits don't have enough funds to meet their demand for services, they can't possibly afford to publicize their good works in an effort to attract new donors. That's why this chapter has introduced you to some of these nonprofits: so that you might consider making a charitable investment in early childhood educational programs. [27]

"What I'd like to see happen is that more private people knew what we were doing and became so inspired by it that they'd want to be a part of it, " emphasized the Quincy Community Action Programs' Anne Leister. Room to Grow's Saskia Epstein similarly commented: "We have the ability to effect change, to really alter the life trajectory of a child. You can look at the research in the health sector, you can look at the research in the mental health sector, you can look at the educational outcomes – all of those ills that we invest so much of our both public and private dollars and resources and society's energy to try to fix later on in life can really be affected through an effort to focus on early childhood and on supporting families during that vulnerable period. So I'm really excited about the growing interest in early childhood. And I think that the more our public awakens to the possibilities that exist in altering the life trajectory of families and of children, and the return on investment – as that is better understood, my hope is that more people will be joining us."

And *my* hope is that you will be one of them. The fact that a high-quality early childhood education can enable low-income children to realize the great promise of upward mobility that has historically been part of the experience of growing up in the United States is a powerful reason to invest in these kids. [28]

Moreover, based on a cost-benefit analysis of what is in our society's long-term interests investing in early childhood enrichment simply makes sense. University of Chicago economist and Nobel Prize winner James Heckman has in recent years been one of the most outspoken champions of universal preschool, arguing that this investment is critical for the future well-being of our economy given the low skill level of U.S. workers relative to others around the world. Heckman and other economists have calculated that every dollar invested in early childhood education can save at least $13 in the long run. Each dollar spent on the High/Scopes Perry Preschool program during the 1960s led to a savings of $12.90. [29]

Investing in early childhood enrichment means more people grow up with the skills to become productive contributors to our society, while at the same time cost savings accrue from reduced spending on crime prevention, imprisonment, special education, public assistance, and health care. We ought to think of this investment in the same way that in the past we have looked at expenditures for highway construction, housing development, and pollution control: as in our long-term economic interests. Heckman has calculated that the societal benefits of spending on early childhood education far exceed the returns we get from investing in adolescents or adults who need skills remediation in order to become productive contributors to the economy (for example, by pursuing their GED or receiving job training). Indeed, it's hard to imagine that *any* type of investment to restore the American dream could yield as many societal advantages as those which move us closer to the reality of providing an enriched early childhood education for all children. [30]

# PART III

# Making a Difference

# 7

# Gifts That Keep On Giving

*Meet Joe and Kate. They live in a picturesque California suburb and asked us to conceal their identity because what their neighbors don't know is that they are on the verge of losing it all. Joe was laid off eight weeks ago. Kate still has her job but $11 an hour doesn't feed a family of four. They use their savings to pay down their credit card and have little cushion. Kate once volunteered at a soup kitchen. On this day, she was the one asking for help for the first time.*

Sharyn Alfonsi offered these words in a chilling 2010 segment on ABC World News. As she spoke, the camera zoomed in on the family's beautiful home located in a pristine suburban neighborhood. Her report was part of a series titled "The Fight for the Middle Class" broadcast as the unemployment rate hovered around 10 percent. The New York Times ran a similar series called "The New Poor" and many other news sources also extensively reported on how the Great Recession was causing lots of once financially secure people to fall on hard times. Layoffs and foreclosures were chiseling away at the middle class.

A 2012 survey by the Pew Charitable Trusts found 85 percent of median-income adults were having greater difficulty maintaining their standard of living compared to a decade ago. Three-quarters were unable to keep six months of emergency savings in the bank and over half had too little income to retire without experiencing a dip in their standard of living. [1]

Shockingly, by age 75 most Americans will have lived in poverty for at least a year. Washington University Professor Mark Rank came across this startling fact after analyzing people's annual earnings over the course of their entire working lives. He found that just over 45 percent had lived in poverty for two years, more than a third for four years, and nearly 30 percent five or more years. These data, which Rank collected several years *before* the Great Recession began in 2007, shatter the popular image of the poor as a minority subculture holding values at odds with the middle-class mainstream. Poverty affects us all. [2]

Even if you never directly experience significant financial hardship, you are still adversely impacted by the fact that millions of Americans do. A report by the Center for American Progress calculated the costs of childhood poverty as roughly $500 billion a year. These costs reverberate throughout the educational, criminal justice, and healthcare systems. [3]

- *Low achievement.* Disadvantages begin early in life. By kindergarten, test scores of literacy and math tend on average to be 60 percent lower among the poorest children than the most affluent. This gap grows during elementary and middle school to the point that students from low-income families are six times likelier to drop out of high school than kids from high-income families. Society bears the brunt of these inequalities because a vast segment of the workforce lacks the skills to contribute productively to our economy. [4]

- *Crime.* Violence is especially pronounced in neighborhoods with high concentrations of poverty because kids are unlikely to see role models of people pursuing conventional pathways to success. Young black males who grow up in low-income communities face particularly strong pressures to identify with toughness and physicality over education. Violence often stands out in their eyes as the only viable ticket to respect. When a critical mass of under-educated youth turns to crime, we expend tremendous sums of money on police and corrections. Living in fear also exacts a heavy price in terms of quality of life. [5]

- *Poor health.* Low-income kids experience higher rates of asthma and lead poisoning than do kids growing up in higher-income neighborhoods. Children from low-income households are also more susceptible to neglect and abuse, given the dire financial stresses their parents endure. Moreover, poor kids are less likely to receive routine medical care. And when they do, it tends to be from a neighborhood or hospital-based clinic rather than a private doctor. The costs of visiting the emergency room, a frequent occurrence for people without health insurance, are astronomical. [6]

Ultimately, we have a choice – to incur these costs or to invest in programs that relieve the strains the economic opportunity divide puts on our educational, criminal justice, and healthcare systems.

"From the earliest days of our founding," President Obama reminded the nation in his 2011 State of the Union address, "America has been the story of ordinary people who dare to dream. That's how we win the future." Just as long-range thinking has been an enduring source of our national strength, so too must we continue to invest in the American dream. Due to rising inequality, it's now more important than ever for private citizens to give in ways that produce ongoing and sustained impacts for people down on their luck. As earlier chapters illustrate, there are many nonprofits around the U.S. that offer those who are struggling the chance to move their lives forward. Enabling them to access employment, housing, and education is the gift that keeps on giving. Through such help, they acquire the tools to get ahead and become more productive contributors to society. [7]

OPRAH'S RISE TO stardom is a tale we all admire. Born to teen parents in Mississippi, she lived her early years in poverty with her grandmother. Then she moved to Nashville to be with her father and subsequently to Milwaukee to live with her mother.

There, she was sexually assaulted several times by family members and ultimately ended up back with her father, who set her on a disciplined course during her adolescent years. Her grandmother had cultivated in her a love of reading and she was a naturally gifted public speaker. At 19, upon being named Miss Black America, she began her broadcasting career at a TV station in Nashville. After a stint as a news anchor in Baltimore, she moved to Chicago to host a morning talk show. Two years later, at the age of 32, she became host of the *Oprah Winfrey Show*. The rest is history. [8]

We all know the script: if one is determined and hard-working, there are no limits to what life has in store. Oprah's story highlights that in America anything is possible. You're probably familiar with other stories like hers – about people born into families with modest means who achieved considerable success. They embody the rags-to-riches tale that is so definitive of our history and culture. Such people are often profiled in popular magazines and are the subject of Hollywood films. Their stories reinforce the widespread belief that personal ambition is what matters most for getting ahead.

One of my favorite New Yorker cartoons exposes the limitations of this belief. It depicts five businessmen huddled together having an informal meeting and is captioned "OK, guys, now let's go out and <u>earn</u> that four hundred times our workers' salaries." Most of us can recognize the dark humor in this cartoon because we find the stark amount of wealth inequality in our society as grossly unfair. Nonetheless, the view that a person earns – and therefore deserves – his lot in life widely persists. A New York Times poll found that most people see getting ahead as within everyone's reach. Regardless of their own backgrounds, respondents indicated hard work is more important to success than coming from a wealthy family or having the right connections. [9]

Media reporting reinforces this belief. Portrayals of the adversity low-income people experience rarely make the news. Thirteen days after Hurricane Katrina, New York Times Public Editor Byron Calame wrote that he'd looked at the paper's coverage of New Orleans during the 10 years prior to the storm. Despite significant reporting about Katrina's devastating effects on low-income people, over those 10 years there had not been a single article focusing on the daily hardships of the city's poor. Even during the Great Recession when many stories chronicled middle-class families suddenly falling on hard times – like the ABC news segment that opened this chapter – the plight of those who chronically struggle to make ends meet didn't become a subject of elevated coverage. [10]

Low-income people mostly appear in news stories about deviant behavior – such as violent crime, drug abuse, child neglect, or welfare dependency. Rather than explore how deviance is often a response to inequality of opportunity, media reports typically present people's hardships as largely of their own making. News stories about teenage pregnancy are a case in point. This issue hits home with so many parents because it feeds anxieties that their daughter's sexual impropriety will send her spiraling on a downward path – dropping out of school, working dead-end jobs, and becoming welfare dependent. Yet, these problems have deeper roots that the news rarely exposes. The reality is about 80 percent of teenage girls who get pregnant have grown up in low-income families. [11]

There is one time during the year when low-income Americans *are* sympathetically in the public eye – between Thanksgiving and the New Year. Since many people equate the holidays with helping the needy, news sources make special fundraising appeals. Reporters chronicle stories of adversity – such as a parent being layed off or an illness sapping family savings – and showcase examples of generosity that is making a difference in these people's lives.

Consider the story of Theone Ferron, which appeared in the New York Times on Christmas Day, 2009. She had just been layed off from her $17,500 a year job without getting severance pay. A single mother living in the Bronx, at the time she was eight months pregnant with her second child. Family members provided emotional support to help Theone cope with her job loss but couldn't afford to assist financially. After months of being unable to find work, she decided to return to school to fulfill her lifelong ambition to become a special education teacher. But, she wasn't able to get a student loan because she had longstanding debt. In addition she was falling behind on her bills. But when Theone met with a social worker from Catholic Charities, she learned that the New York Times Neediest Cases Fund would pay her bills and buy her a computer for school. [12]

News coverage of people aided by holiday giving campaigns depicts them as deserving of help because their hardships are beyond their own capacity to fix. These fundraising appeals are a temporary departure from the dominant characterization of low-income Americans as personally responsible for their own struggles. Consequently, at the end of each year lots of people like Theone get much-needed help. Yet, the reality is that most of the year we do very little to invest in opportunity for our fellow Americans in need. Their struggles for the most part disappear from our minds in early January, not to reappear until we're eating our Thanksgiving dinners. [13]

The fact that for most of the year we see low-income people as largely responsible for their own struggles greatly diminishes our motivation to help them. This is why choosing to support the charities chronicled in this book is an act of tremendous courage. Doing so acknowledges the inconvenient truth that ours is not the land of opportunity so many take it to be, and underscores that in an era when government is unlikely to address this problem giving is essential for restoring the American dream.

Without your help, the prospects for people who are struggling in school, unemployed, or homeless to get ahead are bleak. A century ago, millions of immigrants found on our shores an industrial economy where toiling long hours on a shop floor led to a better life. Ours was a society where a person with just a high school diploma – and often even without one – could land a job that paid well enough to save for a down payment on a home and to send kids to college. Those days are long gone. Most decent-paying work now requires post-secondary training. Due to factories closing and moving overseas, the jobs available to low-skill workers typically pay poorly and offer few mobility prospects. Whereas 60 years ago GM was the largest employer in the U.S and provided many good jobs, the largest employer today – Wal-Mart – is emblematic of an economy in which a family of four with two parents working full-time for minimum wage earns under $31,000 a year. [14]

The good news is you have a critical role to play in effecting change. Stories of personal transformation chronicled in earlier chapters attest that your giving can make a significant difference for people who otherwise have few prospects for getting ahead. You can provide a vital source of help, measurably improve people's lives, and foster opportunity for all.  What greater mark could you leave on the future!

ON A CRISP autumn day in 2005 U2 lead singer Bono met with President George W. Bush for an hour and 40 minutes over lunch. Amidst intermittent banter about the band's upcoming Washington concerts, the two men discussed the possibility of the U.S. giving more development aid to Africa. It wasn't the first time Bono had conferred with the administration's top brass about this issue. In the summer of 2001 he had spoken with National Security Advisor Condoleezza Rice, and the following March traveled with Treasury Secretary Paul O'Neil on a 10-day tour through Ghana, Ethiopia, Uganda, and South Africa. Bono had also met previously with the president, most recently in July 2005 during the G8 Summit in Gleneagles, Scotland where Bush pledged $50 billion in aid to developing countries by 2010, half of it going to African nations.

*Meeting in the Oval Office*

When not dazzling crowds of screaming fans at sold-out arenas and stadiums, Bono is often seen convening with world leaders – a side gig that has become his second day job. He is one of the most visible champions for the plight of the global poor, advocating that wealthy nations give substantial sums of aid to tackle the dire social problems so many people in Africa and around the world experience daily: AIDS, malaria, tuberculosis, unsanitary drinking water, and inadequate educational opportunity. [15]

Although the White House lunch produced no photo-op pronouncements of new aid commitments, there was something telling about the timing of that meeting. It had been just seven weeks since Hurricane Katrina devastated the Gulf Coast, catapulting U.S. poverty into the national spotlight. Amidst harsh criticism for doing too little to help low-income people evacuate in advance of the storm, President Bush began to make his concern for America's poor more palpable. On the evening of September 15th he addressed the nation from Jackson Square, a signature New Orleans landmark located in the heart of the historic French Quarter. He pledged unwavering support and promised that the city would in time be faring better than it was before the storm.

"We will stay as long as it takes to help citizens rebuild their communities and their lives...As all of us saw on television, there is also some deep, persistent poverty in this region as well. And that poverty has roots in a history of racial discrimination, which cut off generations from the opportunity of America. We have a duty to confront this poverty with bold action. So let us restore all that we have cherished from yesterday, and let us rise above the legacy of inequality." [16]

Since the president had become consumed with managing the Katrina disaster, Bono knew better than to push forward with his Africa agenda. In mid-September he told the New York Times Magazine: "I have to be sensitive about putting my hand in America's pocket at a time like this." Yet, just a month later it was again safe for Bono to reach into the Bush administration's coffers. American poverty had receded from the public eye, again becoming the invisible issue it had long been before Katrina.

When the two men met that October afternoon to discuss the abject conditions experienced by poor people around the world, incredibly neither of them mentioned the plight of low-income Americans. What's more, media coverage of the meeting made no mention of this irony. The New York Times Magazine cover story likewise didn't point out the obvious disconnect between all the jockeying Bono was doing on behalf of Africa's poor and the fact that U.S. poverty had recently become a topic of central concern. [17]

Bono is the most popular among a field of celebrities who advocate for impoverished people around the world. Bob Geldof has also become a household name connecting rock music and development aid. He conceived the Live Aid concerts held in 1985 for Ethiopian famine relief as well as the July 2005 Live 8 concerts that were each held in a different G8 country in the days preceding the Gleneagles summit. In addition to the many top-name musicians performing at these concerts, notables who attended or made speeches included Bill Gates, Nelson Mandela, Kofi Anan, Brad Pitt, Cameron Diaz, Justin Timberlake, George Clooney, and Susan Sarandon.

The efforts of celebrities, world leaders, and high-profile philanthropists to make global poverty an issue of significant public concern manifest what the economist Dambisa Moyo calls the "culture of aid." This refers to humanitarian practices grounded in the belief that we, in the West, have a moral responsibility to improve the condition of the world's poor because they are trapped in circumstances beyond their control. There are, by contrast, few prominent spokespersons advocating that we show similar concern for the plight of our own low-income population. How odd it would seem if American concert audiences were to sing out in unison against economic injustice here at home.

This disparity of concern is understandable given that poor people living in the U.S. do not experience the level of deprivation common in many parts of the world. But they still endure the double burden of having the deck stacked against their chances for mobility and having people cast aspersions on them for failing to get ahead. So while it's vital to come to the aid of destitute people around the world, we must not let doing so absolve us of feeling responsible for fostering greater opportunity in our own society. Charity, after all, begins at home. [18]

NATIONAL PUBLIC RADIO came under attack in 2011 as House Republicans sought to eliminate all federal financing. This move stemmed from strong fervor within both parties to find ways to trim the deficit. The campaign gained momentum amidst growing sentiment on the right that public radio has a liberal bias and is therefore undeserving of federal money. Beyond the question of whether the government should or should not fund public radio is the reality that its support comes primarily from listeners. So unless individuals can be motivated to give, government financing doesn't amount to all that much. That's why during fundraising drives local NPR stations frequently mention how every donation gets them closer to reaching a level sufficient to ensure that programming stays on the air. Such information, when combined with reminders that NPR depends on audience support, provides a strong motivation for people to contribute.

And the impetus for listeners to give can become even greater, as a fascinating psychological study discovered. Researchers set up four scenarios which they tested on callers responding to an on-air fundraising appeal. The person answering the phone either: 1) Told the caller someone else had just contributed $75; 2) Told the caller someone else had just contributed $180; 3) Told the caller someone else had just contributed $300; or 4) Made no mention of others' contributions. In all scenarios, the person then asked callers how much they would like to pledge. It turns out mentioning a previous caller's donation mattered a lot. After controlling for factors such as donors' giving history and gender, the researchers found the proportion of people giving $75 was 12 percent higher when a previous contribution of $75 was mentioned compared to when there was no mention made. Nine percent more of the callers who were informed that the prior caller had just given $300 donated $120 compared to those not told at all. [19]

The takeaway message is that people are likelier to contribute more to a cause when they believe others whom they identify with also give at that level. This suggests individuals can be inspired to support *any* cause if doing so enables them to feel part of an "imagined community" that thrives not because of face-to-face interactions but as a result of publicity around an issue about which people deeply care.

This book provides the seeds for a new kind of imagined community – one nurtured by individuals like you who want to invest in America's future. By reading *Giving Hope*, you are part of a movement comprised of people inspired to do what you can to foster greater opportunity for all.

The moment is ripe for this movement to burgeon. Over the coming decades Baby Boomers will bequeath more wealth to their heirs than any prior generation of Americans ever has – an amount estimated to be as high as $41 trillion by 2055. "Today we have more power as private citizens to do public good, both at home and around the world, than citizens in all of human history have ever had," former President Bill Clinton commented a few years ago. We have an unprecedented opportunity to channel our generosity in ways that can affirm and renew our country's longstanding promise of the chance for people to achieve a better life. [20]

# 8

# High-Impact Nonprofits

The 75 nonprofits listed below help struggling Americans gain access to the American dream. Experts have vetted these nonprofits, so you can trust they use their funds efficiently to make a significant impact. Root Cause, a Boston organization that invests in local nonprofits, vetted the ones detailed in Chapters 4-6. Others listed have been supported by groups of donors that fund successful entrepreneurial nonprofits. These include Social Venture Partners, Roberts Enterprise Development Fund, Venture Philanthropy Partners, and A Better Chicago.

## EAST

### Early Childhood Education

Room to Grow enriches the lives of babies born into poverty during their critical first three years of development.

> http://www.roomtogrow.org
> 212-620-7800
> 54 West 21st Street
> New York, NY 10010
>
> **More Impact!**
> Room to Grow is also in Boston.
>
> ***Read in Chapter 6 about the impacts of Room to Grow's work!**

<u>Nurse-Family Partnership</u> is improving the health, well-being and self-sufficiency of first-time, low-income parents and their children. The organization provides education and support during the child's first two years of life.

> http://www.nursefamilypartnership.org
> 704-248-3701
> 601 E 5th Street, Suite 140
> Charlotte, NC 2820

> **More Impact!**
> Nurse-Family Partnership is in 43 states and the U.S. Virgin Islands.

> ***Read in Chapter 6 how this organization helps families!**

## <u>Youth Development</u>

<u>Future Chefs</u> prepares youth for early employment and post-secondary education opportunities in the culinary field and supports them in developing a broad base of transferable skills as they transition into the working world.

> http://www.futurechefs.net
> 617-451-3883
> 560 Albany Street
> Boston, MA 02118

> ***Read in Chapter 5 about Future Chefs' high-impact work!**

<u>Year Up</u> provides young adults with the skills, experience, and support to enable them to reach their potential through professional careers and higher education.

http://www.yearup.org
617-542-1533
93 Summer Street, 5th Floor
Boston, MA 02110

**More Impact!**
Year Up is also in Atlanta, Baltimore, Chicago, Miami, New York City, Providence, San Francisco, Seattle, and Washington DC.

\*\*\*Read in Chapter 5 about Year Up's significant work!

<u>YouthBuild</u> offers high-school dropouts the opportunity to work toward their GEDs and gain job skills by building affordable housing in their communities.

https://youthbuild.org
617-623-9900
58 Day Street
Somerville, MA 02144

**More Impact!**
There are 273 YouthBuild programs in 46 states, Washington, DC, and the U.S. Virgin Islands.

\*\*\*Read in Chapter 2 how YouthBuild helped Joel!

<u>More Than Words</u> empowers youth who are in the foster care system, court involved, homeless, or out of school to take charge of their lives by running a bookstore/cafe.

> <u>http://mtwyouth.org</u>
> 781-788-0035
> 376 Moody Street
> Waltham, MA 02453

> ***Read in Chapter 5 about the significant impacts of More Than Words' work!**

<u>Communities in Schools</u>, the nation's leading dropout prevention organization, offers at-risk students support to help them stay in high school, graduate, and go on to do post-secondary training.

> <u>http://www.cischarlotte.org</u>
> 704-335-0601
> 601 E. 5th Street, Suite 300
> Charlotte, NC 28202

> **More Impact!**
> The Communities in Schools network Extends across 27 states.  Find out the <u>local affiliate nearest you</u>.

<u>Amachi mentoring program</u> offers pathways to opportunity to kids for whom either one or both of their parents are behind bars. This intervention thwarts the likelihood that these kids too will live a life of crime. Mentors meet weekly with a child who has been carefully matched with them.

> <u>http://www.amachimentoring.org</u>
> 2210 S. 71st Street
> Philadelphia, PA 19142

## K-12 Schools

SEED Foundation supports two college-prep, public boarding schools – in Washington DC and in Maryland. These schools immerse kids from underserved communities in a 24-hour learning environment so that they can achieve their full potential.

> http://www.seedfoundation.com
> 202-785-4123
> 1776 Massachusetts Avenue, N.W., Suite 600
> Washington, D.C. 20036

## Post-Secondary Training

College Summit partners with high schools across the country to increase the college enrollment rates of youth from low-income communities.

> http://www.collegesummit.org
> 202-319-1763
> 1763 Columbia Road NW, Second Floor
> Washington, DC 20009
>
> **More Impact!**
> College Summit has offices in 11 states.

## Jobs

Center for Employment Opportunities (CEO) provides employment services to people with recent criminal records who typically face major hurdles finding jobs because employers see them as untrustworthy and unreliable.

> http://ceoworks.org
> 212-422-4430
> 32 Broadway, 15th Floor
> New York, NY 10004

## Housing

HomeStart assists individuals and families move from shelters to permanent housing. Once housed, it continues to help people reintegrate into their communities by providing support services such as money management programs and life skills training.

> http://homestart.org
> 617-542-0338
> 105 Chauncy Street, Suite 502
> Boston, MA 02111

> ***Read in Chapter 4 about how HomeStart helped Dane!**

Massachusetts Housing & Shelter Alliance partners with government, philanthropy, service providers, and businesses to enable homeless people to move into permanent housing, exercise self-determination, and become less dependent on government help.

> http://www.mhsa.net
> 617-367-6447
> 25 Kingston Street, 3R
> Boston, MA 02111

> ***Read in Chapter 4 how the Massachusetts Housing & Shelter Alliance helped Frankie!**

Pine Street Inn, the largest resource for homeless men and women in New England, provides a comprehensive range of services including permanent supportive housing, job training and placement, emergency shelter, and street outreach.

> http://www.pinestreetinn.org
> 617-892-9100
> 444 Harrison Avenue
> Boston, MA 02118

> ***Read in Chapter 4 how Pine Street Inn helped Cheryl!**

Hearth is the only organization in the nation dedicated exclusively to eliminating homelessness among the elderly, the fastest growing group of homeless people.

> http://www.hearth-home.org
> 617-369-1550
> 1640 Washington Street
> Boston, MA 02118

**\*\*\*Read in Chapter 4 how Hearth helped Peter!**

Corporation for Supportive Housing develops, finances, and operates permanent housing for the chronically homeless and provides services to help these individuals move their lives forward.

> http://www.csh.org
> 212-986-2966
> 50 Broadway, 17th Floor
> New York, NY 10004

Workforce Initiative for Supportive Housing offers permanent housing for homeless families, providing a structured set of supportive services that empower struggling families to move from homelessness to self-sufficiency.

> http://www.christchurchcharlotte.org/www/docs/287/
> 704-333-0378
> 500A Spratt Street
> Charlotte, NC 28206

## Comprehensive Services

<u>Action for Boston Community Development</u> provides basic services that empower individuals, families, and communities to overcome poverty, live with dignity, and achieve their full potential.

> http://www.bostonabcd.org
> 617-348-6000
> 178 Tremont Street
> Boston MA 02111
>
> ***Read in Chapter 6 about Action for Boston Community Development's significant work to foster enriched early childhood development!**

<u>Quincy Community Action Programs</u> offers an array of services to help low-income people achieve self-sufficiency.

> http://www.qcap.org
> 617-479-8181
> 1509 Hancock Street
> Quincy, MA 02169
>
> ***Read in Chapter 6 about Quincy Community Action Program's significant work to foster enriched early childhood development!**

# MIDWEST

## Early Childhood Education

Baby Space provides comprehensive services to low-income parents and children from pregnancy until the child reaches 3rd grade. These services include year-round, full-day childcare; parental education; and mental health support.

> http://www.babyspace.org
> 612-729-5171
> 2438 18th Avenue South
> Minneapolis, MN 55404

Ready Readers encourages and inspires preschool children from low-income communities to become readers so that they may enjoy and prosper from this critical lifelong skill.

> http://readyreaders.org
> 314-564-8070
> 1974 Innerbelt Business Center Drive
> St. Louis, MO 63114

## Youth Development

Rock Star Supply Co. brings volunteer tutors to high schools to lend support to teachers so they can more effectively engage their students. These "rock stars" work with at-risk students to help them catch up on assignments and develop a passion for learning.

> http://www.rockstarsupplyco.org
> 612-367-7827
> 2388 University Ave West
> St. Paul, MN 55114

Aim High is an academic enrichment program for 5th-8th graders from economically distressed neighborhoods who have demonstrated the potential to succeed educationally. Students commit to academic achievement, staying in school, and becoming responsible members of society.

>http://www.aimhighstl.org
>314-432-9500
>755 South Price Road
>St. Louis, MO 63124

Youth Opportunities Unlimited provides work and life skills training to 14-19 year-old youth who are at risk of dropping out of high school.

>http://www.youthopportunities.org
>216-566-5445
>1361 Euclid Avenue
>Cleveland, OH 44115

Open Doors Academy nurtures and challenge at-risk adolescents to enable them to reach their full potential through the provision of meaningful out-of-school enrichment programming.

>http://opendoorsacademy.org
>216-229-1900
>3311 Perkins Avenue
>Cleveland, OH 44114

Youth Enrichment Services mentors teens living in public housing and economically disadvantaged communities in order to promote academic improvement, cultural enrichment, career development, and life skills enhancement.

>http://youthenrichmentservices.org
>412-661-7834
>6031 Broad Street, #202
>Pittsburgh, PA 15206

YouthPlaces promotes the positive development of at-risk 12-18 year-olds by providing a safe place for them to engage in a range of activities including recreation, cultural awareness, mentoring, career readiness and academic enrichment.

>   http://www.youthplaces.org
>   412434-0851
>   711 West Commons
>   Pittsburgh, PA 15212

## K-12 Schools

LEARN is a network of public, college prep elementary schools serving nearly 2,300 underserved K-8 students across six campuses in greater Chicago.

>   http://www.learncharter.org
>   773-722-0200
>   1132 S. Homan Avenue
>   Chicago, IL 60624

## Post-Secondary Training

One Million Degrees offers support and guidance to low-income students attending community college so that they will stay focused on school, graduate, and succeed in life.

>   http://www.onemilliondegrees.org
>   312- 920-9605
>   226 W. Jackson #528
>   Chicago, IL 60606

<u>OneGoal</u> is the nation's only teacher-led college persistence organization. It works to make college graduation possible for all students by identifying, training, and supporting the most effective teachers to lead underperforming high school students to reach their full potential and graduate from college.

> http://www.onegoalgraduation.org
> 773-321-2630
> 215 West Superior Street
> Chicago, IL 60654

> **More Impact!**
> OneGoal is also in Houston.

<u>College Bound</u> provides promising high school students from disadvantaged backgrounds with the academic and social support needed to succeed in four-year colleges.

> www.collegeboundstl.org
> 314-361-4441
> 110 North Jefferson
> St. Louis, MO 63103

## <u>Jobs</u>

<u>Urban Alliance</u> gives youth access to experiences for professional growth, preparing them for a life of work and self-sufficiency through paid internships, formal training, and mentorship.

> http://www.theurbanalliance.org
> 312-496-3300
> 29 South LaSalle, Suite 610
> Chicago, IL 60603

> **More Impact!**
> Urban Alliance is also in Baltimore and Washington DC.

Full Cycle is a nonprofit bike shop that employs homeless youth, teaching them bike repair and hands-on business skills including resume writing, interviewing skills, sales, and customer service.

> http://fullcyclebikeshop.org
> 612-824-7581
> 3515 Chicago Avenue South
> Minneapolis, MN 55407

## Housing

Beyond Housing provides affordable housing and homeownership services and also helps with community-wide rebuilding efforts. These efforts empower residents to become leaders of their own neighborhood revitalization efforts.

> http://www.beyondhousing.org
> 314-533-0600
> 4156 Manchester Avenue
> St. Louis, MO 63110

Famicos Foundation provides access to affordable housing and enhances neighborhood quality. It owns and manages over 800 units of housing for families, seniors, the disabled, and formerly homeless individuals.

> http://www.famicos.org
> 216-791-6476
> 1325 Ansel Road
> Cleveland, OH 44106

ACTION (the Allegheny Council to Improve Our Neighborhoods) helps people to become more secure and self-sufficient through the provision of decent, affordable housing, essential supportive services, asset building programs, and educational and employment opportunities.

> http://www.actionhousing.org
> 412-281-2102
> 425 Sixth Avenue, Suite 950
> Pittsburgh, PA 15219

## Community Development

Urban Strategies empowers residents in distressed urban neighborhoods to lead healthy, prosperous lives in thriving, self-sustaining communities. The organization helps communities build safer neighborhoods, better schools, and offers a range of comprehensive human service supports.

> www.urbanstrategiesinc.org
> 314-421-4200
> 720 Olive Street, Suite 2600
> St. Louis, MO 63101

> **More Impact!**
> Urban Strategies is also in Minneapolis, New Orleans, Los Angeles, and San Francisco.

# SOUTHWEST

## Early Childhood Education

Wild Plum Center for Young Children & Families enables low-income kids to overcome as many barriers to their development and education as possible in order to ensure that these kids are prepared to enter kindergarten at age five.

> www.wildplumcenter.org
> 720-652-4779
> 82 21st Avenue, Suite B
> Longmont, CO 80501

Educational First Steps improves the availability and the quality of early childhood education for economically disadvantaged children in the Dallas area.

> www.educationalfirststeps.org
> 214-824-7940
> 2800 Swiss Avenue
> Dallas, TX 75204

## Youth Development

<u>Youth on Their Own</u> enables homeless youth to stay focused on remaining in high school and graduating. Students receive financial assistance, basic needs, and guidance as they work to obtain their diplomas.

> <u>http://yoto.org</u>
> 520-293-1136
> 1443 West Prince Road
> Tucson, AZ 85705

<u>Tucson Youth Development</u> offers educational and employment programs for low-income youth ages 14-21, enabling them to stay in school, graduate and transition into post-secondary education or the workforce. They gain valuable job experience, develop strong work ethics, and achieve their academic, vocational and personal goals.

> <u>http://www.tucsonyouth.org</u>
> 520-623-5843
> 1901 North Stone Avenue
> Tucson, AZ 85705

<u>Family Learning Center</u> has one simple goal: to teach low-income kids of all ages academic and personal skills to increase the likelihood that they will grow up to become self-sufficient and successful in whatever they choose to do.

> <u>www.flcboulder.org</u>
> 303-442-8979
> 3164 34th Street
> Boulder, CO 80301

<u>Colorado Youth at Risk</u> empowers teenagers to make life choices that positively impact their future through community-based mentoring and intensive training.

> http://coyar.org
> 303-623-9140
> 4701 Marion Street
> Denver, CO 80216

<u>America Scores</u> enables youth to lead healthy lives, be engaged students, and have the confidence and character to make a difference in the world. Its programs in partnerships with local schools integrate soccer, poetry and service-learning to foster students' health, academic achievement and civic engagement.

> http://www.americascores.org
> 303-832-5879
> 4900 West 29th Avenue
> Denver, CO 80212

> **More Impact!**
> America Scores is also in Cleveland, Chicago, San Francisco, Washington DC, Dallas, Los Angeles, St. Louis, Milwaukee, New York City, Portland, and Seattle.

<u>PlatteForum</u> teams underserved, at-risk urban youth with master artists in intensive, structured, and long-term creative learning environments. For these youth, who typically have little access to the arts and mentoring relationships, this partnership enables them to confront challenges and make life-changing discoveries about who they are, what they are capable of achieving, and where they belong in the world.

> http://www.platteforum.org
> 303-893-0791
> 1610 Little Raven Street, Suite 135
> Denver, CO 80202

<u>Dallas Community Lighthouse</u> provides support and guidance to low-income youth in grades K-8 to build their self-esteem and encourage them to stay in school. Students receive tutoring in core subjects like math, language arts, and reading; and they also benefit from consistent adult mentorship, which is something they often do not get at home.

> http://www.communitylighthouse.org
> 972-682-5455
> 9090 Skillman Suite 140-B
> Dallas, TX 75243

<u>Trinity River Mission</u> promotes literacy, encourages academic success and develops effective life skills among disadvantaged youth.

> http://www.trinityrivermission.org
> 214-744-6774
> 2060 Singleton Blvd., Suite 104
> Dallas, TX 75212

<u>Genesys Works</u> enhances the life chances of low-income high school students by offering them the opportunity to work in internships at major corporations during their senior year in high school.

> http://www.genesysworks.org
> 713-341-5777
> 601 Jefferson Avenue, Suite 3950
> Houston, TX 77002

> **More impact!**
> There are also sites in Chicago, Minneapolis, and San Francisco.

## K-12 Schools

<u>KIPP Truth Academy</u> is part of a national network of free, open-enrollment, college-prep schools that strive to equip traditionally underserved students with the knowledge, skills, and character traits necessary to succeed in high school, college, and beyond.

> www.kipptruth.org
> 214-375-8326
> 3200 South Lancaster Road, *Suite 230-A*
> Dallas, TX 75216

<u>Yes Prep</u> is living proof that different outcomes are possible when students from low-income communities are given access to high-quality educational opportunities.  It operates 11 schools that serve 7000 students throughout Houston.

> http://yesprep.org
> 281-227-2044
> 13703 Aldine Westfield Road
> Houston, TX 77039

## Housing

<u>Shared Housing Center</u> offers solutions to those experiencing homelessness.  Whether they are single parents with children, people with special needs, or the elderly, the organization offers both transitional and permanent housing as well as services that enable recipients to become more independent.

> www.sharedhousing.org
> 214-821-8510
> 402 N. Good Latimer Expressway
> Dallas, TX 75204

## Comprehensive Services

Transition Resource Action Center provides skill training, access to affordable housing, livable-wage jobs, and a safety net of community support to enable young adults to transition from foster care to independent living.

> http://citysq.org/TRAC
> 214-823-8710
> 511 N. Akard Street, Suite 302
> Dallas, TX 75201

# WEST

## Early Childhood Education

Denise Louie Education Center provides quality early childhood education services to disadvantaged children and their families in order to promote success in school and community.

> http://www.deniselouie.org
> 206-973-1810
> 606 Maynard Ave S. #101
> Seattle, WA 98104

Thrive by Five Washington provides educational supports and enrichment to ensure that kids from lower-income families do not experience deficits during the most critical years of neurological development.

> http://thrivebyfivewa.org
> 206-621-5555
> 1218 Third Avenue, 8th Floor
> Seattle, WA 98101

## **Youth Development**

Access provides education, workforce training, and support services to enable foster-care youth to achieve self-sufficiency and economic independence.

>   http://www.access2jobs.org
>   858-560-0871
>   2612 Daniel Avenue
>   San Diego, CA, 92111

New Avenues for Youth helps homeless youth escape street life by providing for their basic needs and by offering programs that foster growth and independence.

>   http://www.newavenues.org
>   503-224-4339
>   1220 SW Columbia Street
>   Portland, OR 97201

Friends of the Children matches professional mentors with kids who are susceptible to violence, crime, and drug abuse. Mentors work with children from kindergarten through high school.

>   http://wwwfriendsofthechildren.org
>   503-281-6633
>   44 Northeast Morris Street
>   Portland, OR 97212

>   **More impact!**
>   Friends of the Children is also in in Boston, Seattle, and New York City.

Powerful Schools works to reduce the achievement gap by partnering with public schools to promote literacy, the arts, leadership, and after-school programs.

>   http://powerfulschools.org
>   206-722-5543
>   3401 Rainier Avenue South
>   Seattle, WA 98144

Equal Opportunity Schools works to ensure that all students have the chance to succeed in challenging high school courses. It identifies talented students who, due to their family's financial situation, may miss out on this chance. The organization enrolls and supports such students in these classes so that they may achieve their college goals.

> http://eoschools.org
> 206-547-1167
> 999 N. Northlake Way, Suite 268
> Seattle, WA 98103

Summer Search identifies resilient low-income high school students and inspires them to become responsible and altruistic leaders by providing year-round mentoring, life-changing summer experiences, college advising, and a lasting support network.

> http://www.summersearch.org
> 206-729-0911
> 1109 1st Avenue, Suite 205
> Seattle, WA 98101

## K-12 Schools

Synergy Academies is narrowing the achievement gap among children by operating three high-quality public charter schools in South LA, one of the lowest performing districts within the Los Angeles public school system.

> http://www.wearesynergy.org
> 323-459-5463
> P.O. Box 78638
> Los Angeles, CA 90016

Inner City Education Foundation operates charter schools in South Los Angeles that build a culture of high expectations in providing a rigorous college preparatory education.

> http://www.icefps.org
> 323-290-6900
> 5150 W. Goldleaf Circle, Suite 350
> Los Angeles, CA 90056

Audeo Charter School helps kids for whom conventional schooling has failed them and has put them at risk of dropping out.  Its aim is to enable students to reach their full educational potential.

> http://www.audeocharterschool.net
> 858-678-2050
> 10170 Huennekens Street
> San Diego, CA 92121

## Post-Secondary Training

Barrio Logan College Institute enables low-income students, who are traditionally underrepresented in higher education, to pursue a college degree. Programs begin in 3rd grade and continue until college completion.

> www.blci.org
> 619-232-4686
> 1807 Main Street
> San Diego CA, 92113

Reality Changers helps disadvantaged youth become first-generation college students by providing guidance, tutoring, and financial support.

> http://realitychangers.org
> 619-516-2222
> 3810 University Avenue, Suite 300
> San Diego, CA, 92105

Venture Scholars awards scholarships of up to $4,000 to high school seniors who are motivated to attain post-secondary training but are interested in acquiring technical training rather than a four-year liberal arts degree. They may use the scholarship to attend either a community college or training institute, with the goal of entering the workforce upon graduation.

> http://www.stcventurescholars.org
> 221 NW Second Ave, Suite 210
> Portland, OR 97209

College Access Now enables economically disadvantaged youth to pursue the dream of higher education. Students are assisted with test preparation, navigating the application process, securing funding, and staying committed to doing their schoolwork. An underlying aim of this mentoring is to help students see themselves as worthy and capable of succeeding in college.

> http://www.collegeaccessnow.org
> 1700 - 21st Ave South, #201
> Seattle, WA 98144

## Jobs

Chrysalis creates pathways to self-sufficiency for homeless and low-income individuals by providing the resources and support needed to find and retain employment.

> http://changelives.org
> 213-806-6300
> 522 South Main Street
> Los Angeles, CA 90013

Second Chance creates opportunities for those who have
experienced unemployment, poverty, or have spent time behind
bars, offering programs to enable people to overcome these
significant barriers to employment.

> http://www.secondchanceprogram.org
> 619-234-8888
> 6145 Imperial Avenue
> San Diego, CA 92114

Taller San Jose offers job training to undereducated, unemployed
youth, offering them the opportunity to choose from one of four
16-20 week paid training programs in key industry sectors:

> http://www.tallersanjose.org
> 714-543-5105
> 801 N. Broadway
> Santa Ana, CA 92701

## Housing

Community Housing Partnership works with people who would
otherwise be without a home to develop and operate permanent
affordable housing, integrating optional support services, job
training and community organizing.

> http://www.chp-sf.org
> 415-852-5300
> 20 Jones Street, Suite 200
> San Francisco, CA 94102

## Community Development

Coalition for Responsible Community Development leads initiatives to foster a safe and economically vibrant neighborhood where people can thrive.

> http://www.coalitionrcd.org
> 213-743-6193
> 3101 South Grand Avenue
> Los Angeles, CA 90007

## Comprehensive Services

Neighborhood House has been guided by four words for over a century: *Helping Neighbors Help Themselves*. This organization is a resource for low-income people and recent immigrants, enabling them to overcome the challenges in their lives that impede their attaining success and independence through programs for young children, teens, families and seniors alike.

> http://nhpdx.org
> 503-246-1663
> 7780 SW Capitol Highway
> Portland, OR 97219

Metropolitan Family Service builds stronger communities by providing an array of services to parents, kids, and seniors to help them thrive amidst the stresses that come with poverty.

> http://www.metfamily.org
> 503-232-0007, ext. 107
> 1808 Southeast Belmont Street
> Portland, OR 97214

Casa Esperanza assists homeless individuals and families achieve self-sufficiency by helping them access the services they need to transition to stable employment and housing

> http://www.casa-esperanza.org
> 805-884-8481
> P.O. Box 24116
> Santa Barbara, CA 93121

# Acknowledgments

Although writing this book was a solo endeavor, I simply couldn't have done so without others' help. So many people were instrumental in seeing this book from its inception to its completion.

Special thanks go to Susan Musinsky who connected me to many of the nonprofit leaders and recipients whose stories these pages chronicle. I feel indebted to these individuals for graciously giving of their time to share their stories.

Students greatly aided this project. Those who took my charitable giving course, upon reading draft chapters, offered comments that helped me see where the narrative could be strengthened. Several others assisted with the research: Joan Huang, Megan Goossen, Amanda Kirdulis, Rich Wilkins, Amanda McDermott, and Sara White. Their work was supported by grants from the Center for Excellence in Learning, Teaching, Scholarship, and Service at Framingham State University and the Summer Social Science Research Program at Wellesley College.

I'd like to thank colleagues at Framingham State University. Many of the ideas in this book began as conversations Virginia Rutter and I had while exercising at the gym. I'm also deeply appreciative of the enthusiastic support Sociology Chair Sue Dargan and Academic Vice President Linda Vaden-Goad have both consistently given to my work.

Conversations with friends at Congregation Beth El of Sudbury – Dave Learner, Ben Dubrovsky, Alice Waugh, and Carolyn Schwartz – helped shape my core message. Rabbi David Thomas educated me about the importance of giving within Judaism. After hearing me present some of my early ideas from this project, members of Beth El's Tzedakah Hevra inspired me to think in new and creative ways about it.

Thanks to Graham Peck for the many hours of conversation in which he reminded me I was up to something important, showed me how get there, and expressed enthusiasm about my ideas. I'm also deeply appreciative of Don Hoffman's PR insight. He got me thinking about this book's potential marketability, encouraging me to create a blog and use social media.

I'm grateful to Gail Shapiro and Pam Bauer for each impressing on me the benefits of self-publishing. Liz Ridley greatly improved the writing from earlier drafts; I'm lucky to have found an editor who paid such close attention to detail while also being supportive of my larger endeavor. Stacy Cohen helped with formatting the manuscript. Liz Cademy contributed to perhaps the book's most important feature: its cover.

My deepest appreciation goes to my wife Nancy and our children, Arielle and Benjamin. Their day-to-day support goes immeasurably beyond how often I came up with good ideas or wrote eye-opening prose. They are the glue that makes everything else stick.

# Notes

## 1. Second Chances

[1] "Patterns of Household Charitable Giving by Income Group, 2005" (2007), 15.

[2] Singer, *The Life You Can Save* (2009), 19-20; Wagner, *What's Love Got to Do with It?* (2000), 77-79.

[3] This quote from Booker T. Washington can be found at http://www.leadershipnow.com/leadingblog/2011/02/the_wisdom _of_booker_t_washing.html.

[4] Moll et al, "Human Fronto–Mesolimbic Networks Guide Decisions about Charitable Donation" (2006); McClelland and Kirshnit, "The Effect of Motivational Arousal through Films on Salivary Immunoglobulin" (1988).

[5] Katrina damage projections come from Brinkmann and Ragas, "An Estimate of the Cost of Hurricane Katrina Flood Damage to Single-Family Residential Structures in Orleans Parish" (2006); a good source for basic facts about Katrina is Douglas Brinkley, *The Great Deluge* (2006). I also consulted web sites of well-reputed organizations, including the Discovery Channel and National Geographic. See http://dsc.discovery.com/convergence/katrina/facts/facts.html and http://news.nationalgeographic.com/news/2005/09/0906_050906 _katrina_facts_2.html.

[6] This 63 percent figure also includes the two other major hurricanes that occurred in 2005 – Hurricanes Rita and Wilma – and comes from the Conference Board Survey of 5000 Households, April 2006; The $6.5 billion figure is based on data collected by the Indiana University Center on Philanthropy during 2005 and 2006 and reported in *Giving USA* 2006 and *Giving USA* 2007. Statistics about Katrina contributions given to Habitat for Humanity International come from data collected by the Indiana University Center on Philanthropy about total Katrina aid during

the six months after the storm: http://www.philanthropy.iupui.edu/Research/Giving/Hurricane Katrina.aspx. Figures about the number of houses built by New Orleans Area Habitat for Humanity and about its Musicians' Village development come from the organization's web site: http://www.habitat-nola.org/. I interviewed the development director, Gina Stilp, in her New Orleans office in April 2010.

[7] Lewis, *The Four Loves*, 1960.

[8] Wilgoren, "In Tale of Two Families, a Chasm between Haves and Have-Nots" (2005).

[9] Quoted in Wilgoren, "In a Multitude of Forms, the Offers of Help Pour In" (2005).

[10] See Dyson, *Come Hell or High Water* (2005). Even prior to Katrina, a number of commentators had emphasized that there is no such thing as a wholly "natural" disaster: that hurricanes, earthquakes, and the like disproportionately affect those who already live on the margins of society based on their income, race, and where they live. See Cockburn, Clair, and Silverstein, "The Politics of 'Natural' Disaster: Who Made Mitch So Bad?" (1999); Fothergill and Peek, "Poverty and Disasters in the United States: A Review of Recent Sociological Findings" (2004); and Steinberg, *Acts of God* (2000). This perspective became much more pronounced after Katrina since some of the most extensive damage to New Orleans occurred in city's most impoverished neighborhoods. In addition to Dyson's groundbreaking book, see Bates and Swan, *Through the Eye of Katrina* (2007); Hartman and Squires, *There is No Such Thing as a Natural Disaster* (2006); and Marable and Clarke, *Seeking Higher Ground* (2008). For discussions of typical media coverage of American poverty, see Clawson and Trice, "Poverty as We Know It" (2000), 61; Gamson et al "Media Images and the Social Construction of Reality" (1992), 374.

[11] Hertzberg, "Flood Tide" (2005); Data of Americans' contribution to the tsunami relief effort come from the Indiana University Center on Philanthropy and are published in GIVING USA.

Egeland's comments were reported in the Boston Globe article, "Official Fears Drop in Aid for Others" (2005).

12 These writers include Novogratz, *The Blue Sweater* (2010) and Singer, *The Life You Can Save* (2009); The 1.4 billion statistic comes from the World Bank: http://web.worldbank.org/WBSITE/EXTERNAL/TOPICS/EXTPO VERTY/0,,contentMDK:20153855~menuPK:373757~pagePK:148956 ~piPK:216618~theSitePK:336992,00.htm; Rich illustrations of social science research about disasters are Kai Erikson's *Everything in its Path* (1976) and Eric Klinenberg's *Heat Wave* (2002).

13 Congressional Budget Office, "Trends in the Distribution of Household Income Between 1979 and 2007" (2011), http://cbo.gov/ftpdocs/124xx/doc12485/10-25-HouseholdIncome.pdf; Mishel, Bernstein, and Shierholz, "The State of Working America 2008/2009" (2008), 9, http://www.stateofworkingamerica.org/; U.S. Census Bureau, The 2011 Statistical Abstract, http://www.census.gov/compendia/statab/cats/income_expendit ures_poverty_wealth.html; Luhby "Poverty Rate Rises Under Alternate Census Measure" (2011), http://money.cnn.com/2011/11/07/news/economy/poverty_rate/in dex.htm; Tavernise, "Soaring Poverty Casts Spotlight on 'Lost Decade'" (2011), http://www.nytimes.com/2011/09/14/us/14census.html?_r=1&scp= 2&sq=poverty%20increase&st=cse; Yen, "Census shows 1 in 2 people Are Poor or Low-income" (2011), http://finance.yahoo.com/news/census-shows-1-2-people-103940568.html.

14 Schmitt "Inequality as Policy" (2009), retrieved from http://www.cepr.net/documents/publications/inequality-policy-2009-10.pdf, 4; Block, Korteweg, and Woodward, "The Compassion Gap in American Poverty Policy" (2006), 16.

15 Goldberg, *Billions of Drops in Millions of Buckets* (2009), 63-69.

16 A perusal of the *New York Times* in July 2012 is a clear indicator of the timeliness of this topic: see David Brooks, "The

Opportunity Gap" (July 9); Jason DeParle, "Two Classes in America Divided by 'I Do'" (July 14); Joe Nocera "Addressing Poverty in Schools" (July 27); and Peter Edelman, "Poverty in America: Why Can't We End It?" (July 28). Ariely, "Americans Want to Live in a Much More Equal Country (They Just Don't Realize It)" (2012), http://www.theatlantic.com/business/archive/2012/08/americans-want-to-live-in-a-much-more-equal-country-they-just-dont-realize-it/260639/. The Gallup poll was conducted December 16, 2011, http://www.gallup.com/poll/151568/Americans-Prioritize-Growing-Economy-Reducing-Wealth-Gap.aspx; Mazumder, "Upward Intergenerational Mobility in the United States" (2008), 5, http://www.economicmobility.org/assets/pdfs/PEW_EMP_UPWARD_INTERGENERATIONAL.pdf.

[17] The Indiana University/Bank of America study was released in November 2012, http://www.philanthropy.iupui.edu/research-by-category/the-2012-study-of-high-net-worth-philanthropy.


## 2. Thinking Big

[1] "Young, Unemployed and Optimistic" (2012), http://www.pewsocialtrends.org/2012/02/09/young-underemployed-and-optimistic/?src=prc-headline; I interviewed Joel in June 2012..

[2] National Public Radio's All Things Considered, "Oral Histories Show Generosity in Evacuees" (2006).

[3] Peter Grier, "The Great Katrina Migration" (2005).

[4] Jane and Ed Simpson, in interview with the author, Framingham, Massachusetts, May 2010. Their names and the name of the woman who stayed with them, Ajia are pseudonyms.

[5] After the Flood, Stories of Hope, January 12, 2005. http://www.beliefnet.com/Inspiration/2005/01/After-The-Flood-

*Stories-Of-Hope.aspx*; Solnit, *A Paradise Built in Hell* (2009), 204.

[6] Avila and Cancino, "U.S.'s Generosity toward Haiti is Historic But May be Fleeting" (2010); Brooks, "A Nation of Givers" (2008).

[7] These are the giving figures for the four disasters: $2.8 billion after the September 11th terrorist attacks, $1.9 billion in response to the 2004 Indian Ocean tsunami, $1.3 after the 2010 earthquake in Haiti, and an unprecedented $6.5 billion following Hurricane Katrina in 2005. Data for charitable giving after 9/11, the Indian Ocean tsunami, and Hurricane Katrina come from the Indiana University Center on Philanthropy and are published in GIVING USA. Data on donations in response to the earthquake in Haiti come from "How Charities Are Helping Haiti" (2010). The 25 percent figure for the tsunami is from a study done by the Indiana University Center on Philanthropy and reported by Perry, "Donations to Victims of 2004 Asian Tsunami Topped $3-Billion" (2007); the 53 percent figure for the earthquake in Haiti is based on a Fox News poll and reported by Blanton, "Over Half of Americans Contributed to Haiti Victims" (2010); the 63 percent hurricane figure also includes the two other major storms that occurred in 2005 – Hurricanes Rita and Wilma – and comes from the Conference Board Survey of 5000 Households, April 2006; and the 66 percent figure for 9/11 is from Steinberg and Rooney, "America Gives: A Survey of Americans' Generosity After September 11" (2001).

[8] Singer, *The Life You Can Save* (2009), 23; Brooks, "A Nation of Givers" (2008).

[9] *Giving & Volunteering in the United States (2001)*, http://www.cpanda.org/pdfs/gv/GV01Report.pdf; Tocqueville, Democracy in America (1969).

[10] Silver, *Unequal Partnerships* (2006), 15-37.

[11] Patterns of Household Charitable Giving by Income Group, 2005" (2007), 18; *Giving USA* (2011).

[12] Reich, "A Failure of Philanthropy" (2005); Strom, "What Is

Charity?" (2005); Eisenberg, "What's Wrong with Charitable Giving – and How to Fix It." (2009).

[13] This information comes from Indiana University's Center on Philanthropy, *Giving USA* (2006) and was originally reported in the *Chronicle of Philanthropy*. Also see Odendahl, *Charity Begins at Home* (1990).

[14] "Patterns of Household Charitable Giving by Income Group, 2005" (2007), 29; Quoted in Strom, "Big Gifts, Tax Breaks and a Debate on Charity" (2007).

[15] Poppendieck, *Sweet Charity?* (1999), 4; The Feeding America statistics come from its web site: http://feedingamerica.org/about-us.aspx.

[16] The Indiana University/Google survey does not directly show that 2 ½ times as much funding for the poor goes to service provision as for opportunity creation. Rather, I arrived at that figure by delving a bit into the various funding categories the survey tracked: basic needs, religion, health, education, arts, combined purpose, and other causes.

The computation of Katrina aid that went to relieve emergency needs v. rebuilding comes from an analysis of the websites of the 31 organizations that got the most funding, based on data gathered by the Indiana University Center on Philanthropy, and which collectively received 95 percent of the total. My research assistant, Megan Goossen, tracked every single instance mentioned on these organizations' websites of how aid was spent.

[17] "Understanding Donors' Motivations" (2009).

[18] Kennedy, "Selling the Distant Other" (2009), 12; Lowry, *The Construction of "Needy" Subjects* (1998), 76.

[19] Kogut and Ritov, "The Singularity Effect of Identified Victims in Separate and Joint Evaluation (2005); Slovic, "'If I Look at the Mass I will Never Act'" (2007).

[20] Look to the Stars: The World of Celebrity Giving, "Dana Delany Gives The Clothes Off Her Back To Fight Child Hunger" (2010), retrieved from http://www.looktothestars.org/news/4362-dana-delany-gives-the-clothes-off-her-back-to-fight-child-hunger; *Huffington* Post, "Celebs Urge Action Against Hunger" (2010), retrieved from http://www.huffingtonpost.com/2010/02/04/celebs-urge-action-agains_n_450023.html.

[21] Haskell, "Capitalism and the Origins of the Humanitarian Sensibility" (1985), 354-56.

[22] Frank and Cook *The Winner-Take-All Society* (1995); Berger, "Over $1 Trillion to 1 Percent of Charities: How Do We Measure the Results?" (2013), http://www.huffingtonpost.com/ken-berger/nonprofit-effectiveness_b_2701812.html.

## 3. Investing in Opportunity

[1] I learned details about the house at 619 South Alexander Street from the Hands-on New Orleans site coordinator, Peyton Juneau.

[2] This material comes from an interview with Kendra Sampson conducted in Framingham, Massachusetts, May 2012.

[3] All of the material about Boston Cares volunteers comes from interviews conducted by the author in the Boston area between February and early April 2010, just prior to their trip to New Orleans.

[4] I conducted this analysis along with my research assistant, Amanda Kirdulis. We sought out news sources that had a national reach. Although television is a prominent medium of disaster reporting, we opted to look at newspapers because their content is more accessible and easier to track. Comparing coverage in the New York Times and Wall Street Journal offered a rich comparison since the two papers have different political leanings

(the Times more liberal, the Journal more conservative) and different orientations (comprehensive coverage v. mostly financial news). We identified all articles that matched a keyword search for "Hurricane Katrina." They spanned national coverage, business, sports, editorials, op-eds, and letters to the editor. A similar pattern to what we observed with Katrina coverage occurred after the 2010 earthquake in Haiti; see "On the Media" with Bob Garfield, January 29, 2010, http://www.onthemedia.org/transcripts/2010/01/29/03.

[5] Thomaselli, "New Orleans Is a Super Bowl Winner Thanks to Saints" (2010), http://adage.com/article/special-report-super-bowl-2010/orleans-a-super-bowl-winner/141988/; In retrospect, the Saints' championship hardly seems so glorious. A 2012 National Football League investigation found that certain defensive players had been receiving bounties for injuring opposing teams. This revelation led to coach Sean Payton's being suspended for a year without pay. See Battista, "Saints Coach Is Suspended for a Year Over Bounties" (2012), http://www.nytimes.com/2012/03/22/sports/football/nfl-delivers-harsh-punishment-to-saints-over-bounty-program.html?scp=5&sq=saints%20bounty&st=cse.

[6] Wagner and Edwards, "New Orleans by the Numbers" (2007), 168.

[7] For evidence indicating that hurricanes, earthquakes, tsunamis, and tornadoes are not merely natural disasters, see Cockburn, Clair, and Silverstein, "The Politics of 'Natural' Disaster: Who Made Mitch So Bad?" (1999); Fothergill and Peek, "Poverty and Disasters in the United States: A Review of Recent Sociological Findings" (2004); Steinberg, Acts of God (2000); Bates and Swan, Through the Eye of Katrina (2007); Dyson, Come Hell or High Water (2006); Hartman and Squires, There is No Such Thing as a Natural Disaster (2006); and Marable and Clarke, Seeking Higher Ground (2008).

[8] Rich, "Jungleland" (2012).

[9] Data about the link between tsunami coverage and giving come

from research by Brown and Minty, "Media Coverage and Charitable Giving After the 2004 Tsunami" (2008); on the link between media coverage of disaster and the charitable response, also see Bennett and Kottasz, "Emergency Fund-Raising for Disaster Relief" (2000) and Oosterhoff, Heuvelman, and Peters, "Donation to Disaster Relief Campaigns" (2009). The two women quoted, whose names I have changed, are part of a sample of people in Framingham, Massachusetts whom I interviewed in February 2010 about their recent contributions to the relief effort in Haiti.

[10] These news segments come from a promotional DVD compiled by the Salvation Army's National Public Relations Director, Jennifer Byrd.

[11] Data about top recipients of Katrina aid come from the Indiana University Center on Philanthropy for contributions made through February 2006 (http://www.philanthropy.iupui.edu/Research/Giving/Hurricane_Katrina.aspx) as well as data reported in *Giving USA 2006* for contributions made through June 2006. The Center on Philanthropy also tracked the 10-day contributions in response to Katrina and 9/11 – see MacDonald, "Donors Favor Those 'Worthy' of Compassion" (2005); the figures for the earthquake in Haiti and the tsunami come from data compiled by the *Chronicle of Philanthropy* and reported in "Donations to Aid Haiti Exceed $380-Million, Chronicle Tally Finds" (2010); the tsunami amount spans a nine-day time period.

[12] The computation of Katrina aid that went to relieve emergency needs comes from an analysis of the websites of the 31 organizations that got the most funding, based on data collected by the Indiana University Center on Philanthropy, and which collectively received 95 percent of the total. My research assistant, Megan Goossen, tracked every single instance mentioned on these organizations' websites of how Katrina aid was spent. Data about volunteers come from interviews I conducted in 2010 in both Washington, DC and New Orleans with people at nonprofits centrally involved in the Katrina relief and recovery effort.

[13] This video can be found at http://www.youtube.com/watch?v=kTY4-K3Z1Vw.

[14] This material comes from an interview with Susan Musinsky conducted in Cambridge, Massachusetts, February 2011.

[15] This material comes from a phone interview with Toni Elka, May 2011.

[16] This material comes from a phone interview with Jodi Rosenbaum, May 2011.

[17] These statements come from "Social Impact Report Card" (undated).

## 4. Returning Home

[1] This material is from a presentation Dane gave in October 2011 at Framingham State University as part of the Homelessness Speakers' Bureau and a follow-up interview in June 2012.

[2] "Social Issue Report: Ending Chronic Homelessness" (2011), 2, http://rootcause.org/documents/Homelessness-Issue.pdf; Bornstein, "A Plan to Make Homelessness History" (2010), http://opinionator.blogs.nytimes.com/2010/12/20/a-plan-to-make-homelessness-history/; The exact count of the chronically homeless is 99,894, based on a January 2012 survey by the U.S. Department of Housing and Urban Development reported in Lowrey, "Homeless Rates in U.S. Held Level Amid Recession, Study Says, But Gains Are Elusive" (2012), http://www.nytimes.com/2012/12/10/us/homeless-rates-steady-despite-recession-hud-says.html?_r=0.

[3] "Social Issue Report: Ending Chronic Homelessness," 3-4; Sermons, "A Focus on Chronic Homelessness" (2011), http://www.rootcause.org/blog/guest-blog-a-focus-chronic-homelessness.

4 Ofstehage, "A Solution to Ending Chronic Homelessness" (2011), http://www.rootcause.org/blog/a-solution-ending-chronic-homelessness; "Social Issue Report: Ending Chronic Homelessness"(2011), 4.

5 Bornstein, "A Plan to Make Homelessness History" (2010).

6 Gladwell, "Million Dollar Murray" (2006), http://gladwell.com/2006/2006_02_13_a_murray.html.

7 Interview with Erin Donohue, March 2011; Numbers come from the Massachusetts Housing and Shelter Alliance website, http://www.mhsa.net/matriarch/default.asp.

8 Interview with Erin Donohue; Maslow, "A Theory of Human Motivation" (1943), http://psychclassics.yorku.ca/Maslow/motivation.htm.

9 Frankie's story is recounted in the Massachusetts Housing and Shelter Alliance blog posting on March 2, 2011 – http://jointhehousingrevolution.wordpress.com/2011/03/02/keys-cure-homelessness-an-inspiring-true-story/. The broader successes of eradicating chronic homelessness in Worcester are chronicled in "Social Issue Report: Ending Chronic Homelessness" (2011), 2.

10 Edens, Mares, and Rosenheck, "Chronically Homeless Women Report High Rates of Substance Use Problems Equivalent to Chronically Homeless Men" (2011), http://www.ncbi.nlm.nih.gov/pubmed/21703865; This percentage comes from research reported on the National Network to End Domestic Violence Website, http://www.nnedv.org/policy/issues/housing.html.

11 This material is from a presentation Cheryl gave in October 2011 at Framingham State University as part of the Homelessness Speakers' Bureau and a follow-up interview in June 2012. Other information about Pine Street Inn comes from Johnson, "From a Shelter to a Place Called Home" (2011),

http://www.boston.com/news/local/massachusetts/articles/2011/0
1/10/from_a_shelter_to_a_place_called_home/ and the
organization's website, http://www.pinestreetinn.org/.

[12] Peter's story draws from a piece in the Boston Herald on May 17,
2008
(http://bostonherald.com/news_opinion/local_coverage/2008/05/
senior_and_his_paintings_find_home_thanks_hub_program), a
New England Cable News segment on August 11, 2008
(http://www.hearth-
home.org/news/pr/seniors_recover_golden_years.html#.UNCW5
uSoqSo), and a profile by the local CBS affiliate on November 30,
2008 (http://www.hearth-home.org/news/pr/cbs-11-30-
08.html#.UNCTieSoqSo).  Information about Spencer house can
be found at http://www.rogerson.org/SpencerHouse.php.
Information about Hearth comes from the following sources:
Rosso, "Formerly Homeless Seniors Find New Home and
Community in Mattapan" (2012),
http://www.boston.com/yourtown/news/dorchester/2012/06/hold
_formerly_homeless_seniors.html?camp=pm; a 2011 joint
interview I conducted with President & CEO Mark Hinderlie and
Director of Institutional Advancement Annie Gamey; the
organization's website (http://www.hearth-home.org/index.html);
the four-page prospectus it developed when it was a Social
Innovator; annual reports from 2009 and 2010; and various
brochures.

[13] "Opening Doors: Federal Strategic Plan to Prevent and End
Homelessness" can be found at
http://www.ich.gov/PDF/OpeningDoors_2010_FSPPreventEndHo
meless.pdf; "Social Issue Report: Ending Chronic Homelessness"
(2011), 2; Lowrey, "Homeless Rates in U.S. Held Level Amid
Recession, Study Says, But Gains Are Elusive" (2012); "Out of
Reach: America's Forgotten Housing Crisis" can be found at
http://www.beyondshelter.org/aaa_initiatives/ending_homelessn
ess.shtml.

[14] "Out of Reach: America's Forgotten Housing Crisis" (2012),
http://nlihc.org/sites/default/files/oor/2012-OOR.pdf, 1-4.

[15] The Colorado study is discussed in "Social Issue Report: Ending Chronic Homelessness" (2011), 5; Data in the graph about average annual cost savings per person come from the Massachusetts Housing and Shelter Alliance, http://www.mhsa.net/matriarch/MultiPiecePage.asp_Q_PageID_E_57_A_PageName_E_WhatwedoHomeandHealthyforGood.

## 5. Developing Young Talent

[1] This material is from a phone interview with Aquila, July 2011. The photo is © Laura Widness and used by permission.

[2] Fry, "College Enrollment Hits All-Time High" (2009), 3, http://pewsocialtrends.org/files/2010/10/college-enrollment.pdf.

[3] "Pathways to Prosperity" (2011), http://www.gse.harvard.edu/news_events/features/2011/Pathways_to_Prosperity_Feb2011.pdf, 2-3, 23-37; "Social Issue Report: Workforce Development" (2011), 2. Carnevale, Jayasundera, and Hanson, "Five Ways That Pay Along the Way to the B.A." (2012), 5, http://www9.georgetown.edu/grad/gppi/hpi/cew/pdfs/CTE.Five Ways.ExecutiveSummary.pdf.

[4] Shipler, *The Working Poor* (2005), 126-27; Kirchenman and Neckerman, "'We'd love to Hire Them, But...'" (1998); Wilson, *When Work Disappears* (1996).

[5] "Social Issue Report: Workforce Development (2011), 3 http://rootcause.org/documents/WFD-Issue.pdf; Shipler, 7.

[6] Reich and Wimer, "Has the Great Recession Made Americans Stingier?" (2009), http://www.stanford.edu/group/scspi/_media/pdf/pathways/fall_2011/PathwaysFall11_Reich.pdf.

[7] This material comes from a phone interview with Toni Elka, May 2011.

[8] Material here comes from the 4-page pitch Future Chefs developed when it was a Root Cause Social Innovator in 2011; "Restaurant Industry: The Economy's Best Friend (2011), http://www.qsrmagazine.com/news/restaurant-industry-economys-best-friend.

[9] This information comes from Future Chefs' web site: http://www.futurechefs.net/.

[10] This information comes from Year Up's web site: http://www.yearup.org/; Bornstein.

[11] Shining City interview with Gerald Chertavian, October 2010, http://www.shiningcity.tv/node/261; The quote from Chertavian comes from Year Up's web site.

[12] This information comes from More Than Words' web site, http://mtwyouth.org/, and from the 4-page pitch the organization developed when it was a Root Cause Social Innovator in 2009.

[13] This material comes from a phone interview with Jodi Rosenbaum, May 2011.

[14] Brian's story is recounted in the 4-page pitch that More Than Words developed when it was a Root Cause Social Innovator in 2009.

[15] Rebecca's story is recounted on More Than Words' web site.

[16] The material is from a phone interview with Aly, July 2011.

[17] Future Chefs' success indicators come from the 4-page pitch it developed when it was a Root Cause Social Innovator; Year Up's success indicators are reported on the organization's web site and in Roder and Elliot, "A Promising Start" (2011), http://www.economicmobilitycorp.org/uploads/A%20Promising%20Start.pdf.

[18] Data about More Than Words comes from its web site and the 4-page pitch the organization developed when it was a Root Cause

Social Innovator.

[19] Lareau, *Home Advantage* (2000); MacLeod, *Ain't No Makin' It* (2008).

[20] The quote from Zuleimy is from an interview conducted in Boston, July 2011; Sherley's story is recounted on Year Up's web site.

[21] Bornstein, "Training Youths in the Ways of the Workplace;" Holzer, "Workforce Development as an Antipoverty Strategy" (2009), 62-63, http://www.irp.wisc.edu/publications/focus/pdfs/foc262k.pdf.

[22] President Obama's February 2009 speech was reprinted in the Los Angeles Times, http://latimesblogs.latimes.com/washington/2009/02/obama-text-spee.html; He touted Year Up at a press conference broadcast on CNBC, http://www.youtube.com/watch?v=e3Yf9sse-8; The 2009 speech announcing his community college initiative is at http://www.whitehouse.gov/the_press_office/Excerpts-of-the-Presidents-remarks-in-Warren-Michigan-and-fact-sheet-on-the-American-Graduation-Initiative/; Greenblatt, "For Community Colleges, a Hard Lesson in Politics (2010), http://www.npr.org/templates/story/story.php?storyId=125225059; The 2011 speech announcing an expansion of the community college initiative is at http://www.whitehouse.gov/the-press-office/2011/06/08/president-obama-and-skills-americas-future-partners-announce-initiatives.

[23] "Pathways to Prosperity," 4; Shining City interview with Gerald Chertavian, October 2010; Information about Year Up's support from sponsoring companies comes from Michael Goldstein in an interview with the author, Framingham, Massachusetts, May 2011; Bornstein, "Training Youths in the Ways of the Workplace."

[24] "Social Issue Report: Workforce Development," 4; Henderson, MacAllum, and Karakus, "Workforce Innovations" (2010), http://www.nyc.gov/html/ceo/downloads/pdf/workforce_programs_evaluation_report.pdf; Britt, "Crime and Unemployment

among Youths in the United States", (1994).

## 6. Getting the Right Start

[1] This family's story is chronicled on the Nurse-Family Partnership website, http://www.nursefamilypartnership.org/First-Time-Moms/Stories-from-moms/Antoinette-s-story; Additional information about the organization comes from Leland, "Someone to Lean On" (2012), http://www.nytimes.com/2012/12/16/nyregion/nyc-nurses-aid-low-income-first-time-mothers.html?pagewanted=all&_r=0.

[2] Public opinion about the stimulus package comes from a November 2011 Reuters poll, where 62% of respondents expressed that this spending did little to help the economy and at the same time added to the federal debt – http://www.ipsos-na.com/news-polls/pressrelease.aspx?id=5397; Probably the most vocal source of support for the stimulus among economists comes from Mark Zandi, a political moderate, who is Senior Economist at Moody's Analytics – see http://www.usatoday.com/money/economy/2010-08-30-stimulus30_CV_N.htm.

[3] "Basic Head Start Facts," retrieved from National Head Start Association website: www.nhsa.org; Action for Boston Community Development website: http://www.bostonabcd.org/.

[4] This material comes from a phone interview with Anne Leister and Keather Reickle, August 2011.

[5] Halle et al, "Disparities in Early Learning and Development: Lessons from the Early Childhood Longitudinal Study" (2009), retrieved from http://www.childtrends.org/Files/Child_Trends-2009_07_10_FR_DisparitiesEL.pdf, 2-4; National Center for Children in Poverty, Annie E. Casey Foundation, "Child Poverty Still on the Rise, but Outlook for Children Better in Education and Health, KIDS COUNT Report Finds" (2013), http://www.aecf.org/Newsroom/NewsReleases/HTML/2013/Child PovertyStillontheRise.aspx.

[6] Hart and Risley, "The Early Catastrophe" (2003); "Social Issue Report: School Readiness (2010), 2.

[7] This material comes from a phone interview with Anne Leister and Keather Reickle, August 2011.

[8] Hechinger Report, "Pre-K Issues Step to the Front of the Classroom" (2010), http://hechingerreport.org/content/pre-k-issues-step-to-the-front-of-the-classroom_2007/.

[9] Head Start Impact Study Annual Report (2010), http://www.acf.hhs.gov/programs/opre/hs/impact_study/reports/impact_study/hs_impact_study_final.pdf, xxv.

[10] Kozol, "Still Separate, Still Unequal" (2005), 44; Kozol, "Savage Inequalities" (2000).

[11] Data about the "fade" in test scores comes from Currie and Thomas, "School Quality and the Longer-term Effects of Head Start" (1999), http://www.econ.ucla.edu/people/papers/currie/schqual.pdf; Interview with Chris Sieber, July 2011.

[12] Interview with Chris Sieber, July 2011; Chetty et al., "How Does Your Kindergarten Classroom Affect Your Earnings?" (2011).

[13] Calman and Tarr-Whelan, "Early Childhood Education for All: A Wise Investment" (2005), http://web.mit.edu/workplacecenter/docs/Full%20Report.pdf, 12.

[14] Ibid, 13-14.

[15] Van Galen, "Maintaining Control: The Structure of Parent Involvement" (1987).

[16] Lareau, *Home Advantage* (2000), 114-16, 176-80.

[17] Information about how Head Start increases parents' involvement in their children's education comes from the website

for Action for Boston Community Development: http://www.bostonabcd.org/head-start-early-childhood-education.aspx.

[18] Interview with Chris Sieber, July 2011.

[19] "Basic Head Start Facts," retrieved from National Head Start Association website: www.nhsa.org; Action for Boston Community Development website: http://www.bostonabcd.org/.

[20] DiLauro, "Learning, Thriving, and Ready to Succeed" (2010), http://main.zerotothree.org/site/DocServer/EHSsinglesMar5.pdf?docID=7884, Early Childhood Highlights (2010), http://www.childtrends.org/Files/Child_Trends-2010_06_18_ECH_SchoolReadiness.pdf, 2.

[21] "Basic Head Start Facts," retrieved from National Head Start Association website: www.nhsa.org; "Social Issue Report: School Readiness (2010), 1.

[22] Larson, "Room To Grow" (2011), 53-55, http://issuu.com/exhalelifestyle/docs/exhale_summer_2011.

[23] Wilson, "2011 Family Advocate of the Year", 29, http://boston.parenthood.com.

[24] Taniesha Henry is quoted in Larson, 55.

[25] These percentiles come from Room To Grow's website: www.roomtogrow.org; Phone interview with Saskia Epstein, September 2011.

[26] Summaries of these 2003 studies of public attitudes toward Head Start are posted on the National Head Start Association website: www.nhsa.org; More recent public opinion data come from a 2007 Democracy Corp poll (http://www.stateinnovation.org/Research/Education/Universal-Pre-K/democorp_poll_2007.aspx) and a 2008 Hart Research/American Viewpoint poll (http://www.stateinnovation.org/Research/Education/Universal-

Pre-K/Pre-K_Now_poll_release.aspx).

27 "Basic Head Start Facts;" Goldberg, Billions of Drops in Millions of Buckets (2009), 66-67; "Social Issue Report: School Readiness (2010), 4-5.

28 Phone interview with Saskia Epstein, September 2011.

29 "Early Childhood Education for All: A Wise Investment" (2005) 2, 13, 16.

30 "Social Issue Report: School Readiness" (2010), 6, http://rootcause.org/documents/SR-Issue.pdf; "Early Childhood Education for All: A Wise Investment" (2005) 11, 16.

## 7. Gifts That Keep On Giving

1 ABC World News with Diane Sawyer, "Economic Troubles Push Some Middle-Class Americans to the Edge of Poverty" (2010), http://abcnews.go.com/WN/americas-middle-class-families-edge/story?id=10116754; The survey "The Lost Decade of the Middle Class" can be found at http://www.pewsocialtrends.org/2012/08/22/the-lost-decade-of-the-middle-class/.

2 Rank, One Nation, Underprivileged (2005), 91-96, 106.

3 Holzer, Schanzenbach, Duncan, and Ludwig, "The Economic Costs of Poverty" (2007).

4 Lee and Burkam, "Inequality at the Starting Gate" (2002); Cordes and Miller, "Inequality of Education in the United States" (n.d.), http://cte.rockhurst.edu/s/945/images/editor_documents/content/PROJECT%20INEQUALITY%20STUDENT%20PAPERS(Listed%20Alphabetically%20by%20P/cordes.pdf; Walpole, "Socioeconomic Status and College" (2003).

5 MacLeod Ain't No Makin' It (2008); Anderson, Code of the Street

(1999); Krivo and Peterson, "Extremely Disadvantaged Neighborhoods and Urban Crime" (1996).

[6] Manson and Bassuk, "Obesity in the United States" (2003); Halfon and Newacheck, "Childhood Asthma and Poverty" (1993); Drake and Pandey, "Understanding the Relationship between Neighborhood Poverty and Specific Types of Child Mistreatment" (1996); Wood, "Effect of Child and Family Poverty on Child Health in the United States" (2003).

[7] A transcript of President Obama's 2011 State of the Union address can be found at http://www.npr.org/2011/01/26/133224933/transcript-obamas-state-of-union-address.

[8] Oprah's story is chronicled on many websites including her own. This synopsis is from http://www.icmrindia.org/free%20resources/casestudies/Oprah%20Winfrey2.htm and http://sun.menloschool.org/~sportman/ethnic/individual/winfrey/index.html.

[9] The cartoon appeared in the April 24, 2000 *New Yorker*; Ariely, "Americans Want to Live in a Much More Equal Country (They Just Don't Realize It)" (2012), http://www.theatlantic.com/business/archive/2012/08/americans-want-to-live-in-a-much-more-equal-country-they-just-dont-realize-it/260639/; New York Times, "How Class Works" (2005), http://www.nytimes.com/packages/html/national/20050515_CLASS_GRAPHIC/index_04.html.

[10] Calame, "Covering New Orleans: The Decade before the Storm" (2005). He did come across a November 2000 feature story that included vivid descriptions of poverty and its devastating effects, but this discussion did not appear until the article's 16th paragraph. Reading that deeply into a news story is beyond the attention span of most media audiences these days. DeMause, "The Recession and the Deserving Poor" (2009), http://fair.org/extra-online-articles/the-recession-and-the-deserving-poor/.

[11] Iyengar, "Framing Responsibility for Political Issues" (1990), 23; Luker, *Dubious Conceptions* (1996), 107; Males, "Behaving Like Children" (2011).

[12] Haskell, "No Work, Two Children and a Mounting Pile of Bills" (2009).

[13] Edelman, "Forgotten Stories about Forgotten People" (2001); Kendall, *Framing Class* (2005), 94-95, 124-28; Loseke, "The Whole Spirit of Modern Philanthropy" (1997), 429-30.

[14] Block, Korteweg, and Woodward, "The Compassion Gap in American Poverty Policy" (2006), 14-15; Heiner, Social Problems (2013), 55; "America's 5 Biggest Employers Then and Now (2010), http://www.huffingtonpost.com/2010/09/23/americas-5-biggest-employ_n_736215.html#s143988&title=1_General_Motors; Luhby "Poverty Rate Rises Under Alternate Census Measure" (2011), http://money.cnn.com/2011/11/07/news/economy/poverty_rate/index.htm; Tavernise, "Soaring Poverty Casts Spotlight on 'Lost Decade'" (2011), http://www.nytimes.com/2011/09/14/us/14census.html?_r=1&scp=2&sq=poverty%20increase&st=cse.

[15] Peterson, "Bono Visits Bush at the White House" (2005), retrieved from http://today.msnbc.msn.com/id/9755936; Traub, "The Statesman" (2005).

[16] A complete transcript of Bush's Jackson Square speech can be found at http://rebuildinggulfcoast.com/bush.html.

[17] Quoted in Traub (2005).

[18] Moyo, *Dead Aid* (2009), xviii; Lowry, *The Construction of "Needy" Subjects* (1998), 53.

[19] Shang and Croson, "Field Experiment in Charitable Contribution (2009); Anderson, *Imagined Communities* (1983).

[20] Havens and Schervish, *A Golden Age of Philanthropy?* (2006),

http://www.bc.edu/research/cwp/features/goldenage/_jcr_content/; William J. Clinton Foundation Annual Report (2006), http://www.clintonfoundation.org/.

# About the Author

Ira Silver has spent his career investigating how giving can create lasting social change. He blogs at www.oppforall.com about nonprofits that offer second chances to Americans experiencing hard times.

He is Professor of Sociology at Framingham State University and Visiting Professor of Sociology at Wellesley College, having received his BA *summa cum laude* from Amherst College and his Masters and Ph.D. from Northwestern University. He has authored or edited three previous books.